The Hotchkiss Map of the Shenandoah Valley

The Handley Library, Winchester, Virginia

Alexander Neil
and the
Last Shenandoah Valley Campaign

࿊

Dr. Alexander Neil

Franklin County
(Columbus, Ohio:
Historical Publishing
Company,
1901)

Alexander Neil
and the
Last Shenandoah Valley Campaign

৵

*Letters of an
Army Surgeon to his Family, 1864*

Edited by Richard R. Duncan

White Mane Publishing Company, Inc.

This White Mane Publishing Company, Inc. publication was printed by
Beidel Printing House, Inc.
63 West Burd Street
Shippensburg, PA 17257 USA

In respect for the scholarship contained herein, the acid-free paper used in this
book meets the guidelines for permanence and durability of the Committee on
Production Guidelines for Book Longevity of the Council on Library Resources.

For a complete list of available publications
please write
White Mane Publishing Company, Inc.
P.O. Box 152
Shippensburg, PA 17257 USA

Library of Congress Cataloging-in-Publication Data

Neil, Alexander, 1838-1901.
    Alexander Neil and the last Shenandoah Valley campaign : letters
of an army surgeon to his family, 1864 / edited by Richard R. Duncan.
        p.   cm.
    Includes bibliographical references and index.
    ISBN 0-942597-95-8 (alk. paper)
    1. Neil, Alexander, 1838-1901--Correspondence. 2. Shenandoah
Valley Campaign, 1864 (May-August)--Personal narratives.
3. Shenandoah Valley Campaign, 1864 (August-November)--Personal
narratives. 4. Shenandoah Valley Campaign, 1865--Personal
narratives. 5. United States. Army. West Virginia Infantry
Regiment, 12th (1862-1865) 6. United States. Army--Surgeons-
-Correspondence. I. Duncan, Richard R.   II. Title.
E476.66.N45   1996
973.7'37--dc20   96-26375
                                                                CIP

PRINTED IN THE UNITED STATES OF AMERICA

Table of Contents

Preface

The summer of 1863 was not only a critical and crucial one for the American Union, but a decisive one for Alexander Neil, then a young recent graduate of the Cincinnati College of Medicine and Surgery. The Civil War raged that summer with increased severity. For Unionists it was a period of intense excitement, despondency and then jubilation. A Union army under General Ulysses S. Grant was seemingly stalemated before Vicksburg on the Mississippi River, while in the East General Robert E. Lee and the Army of Northern Virginia marched into Pennsylvania. Confederate hopes and expectations soared, but suddenly the Southern euphoria of that summer was shattered in early July. Three days of fierce fighting at Gettysburg sent the Confederate army reeling back to the Rappahannock-Rapidan line in Virginia. Simultaneously in the West, Vicksburg fell to Grant's persistent efforts. The stunning victories electrified Unionists and Alexander Neil.

Caught up in the excitement, Neil went to Wheeling, West Virginia, to see Governor Arthur I. Boreman in late July. He hoped to secure a surgeon's commission in one of that state's regiments. However, patriotism was not his sole reason. From Wheeling he instructed his parents to write to D. W. Rhodes of Louisville, Kentucky, thanking him "for his kindness in giving me the job," but also to inform him "that I came to Virginia on a visit & Gov. Boreman offered me a commission in the army which I could [not] refuse as the draft was imminent at home." Neil, securing the necessary requisition from the governor, was examined by a medical board which at the conclusion of its interrogation recommended his appoint-

ment as a regimental surgeon. He was delighted with his perfor-
mances. Excitedly he wrote home that "It seemed as though the
Board could not stall me, my mind was so unusually bright. They
told me that they were highly pleased with my competency . . ."
Unfortunately for Neil, the only vacancy then existing was that of an
assistant surgeon. He readily accepted an assignment with the 12th
West Virginia Regiment. Jubilant, Neil immediately telegraphed the
news to his parents: "I was commissioned this day Surgeon in the
Potomac Army Send forty (40) dollars by Express."[1]

Although an Ohioan by birth, Neil had Virginia roots. His parents came to Ohio from that state, and an uncle lived in the Wheeling area. His mother, Elizabeth Walker, was the daughter of John
Walker, a native of Ireland who had settled in Virginia and moved to
Ohio in 1832. Neil's father, Charles, also a Virginian, settled in Delaware County in the same year and later married Walker's daughter.
Initially Charles Neil ran an ashery and taught school. In 1824 he
entered politics and was elected county surveyor, an office he held
until 1864. In that year he was elected county auditor; after serving
two terms he became mayor of Delaware.[2]

Alexander Neil, one of his four sons, was born in Eden on December 21, 1838.[3] After receiving his early education in the schools
of Delaware County, Neil entered Ohio Wesleyan University where
he received his bachelor's degree in 1858. He then went to Cincinnati to enroll in the Medical College of Ohio and the Cincinnati College of Medicine and Surgery. He studied under Dr. George C.
Blackman, a nationally prominent surgeon and a fellow of the Royal
College of Surgeons of London, who had to his credit several mono-
graphs on surgery, a translation of *Vidal on Syphilis*, and an edition
of Velpeau's *Operative Surgery*.[4] Interested in surgery, Neil received
his medical degree from the Cincinnati College of Medicine and Surgery in 1863.[5]

With commission in hand Neil joined his regiment at
Sharpsburg, Maryland, on August 2nd. The 12th West Virginia,
organized in 1862 and composed of men from what was then western Virginia, was initially used to protect that region and to guard
the very important Baltimore and Ohio Railroad against Southern
attacks and depredations.[6] Duty along the railroad, except for guer-
rilla activities and an occasional raid, had the tedium of garrison
life. But the resumption of military campaigning in the spring of
1864 radically changed Neil's and the 12th West Virginia's life of
ennui.

With Grant in command as general-in-chief of Union armies,
the Shenandoah Valley and western Virginia became an important
and integral part of Grant's overall strategy of applying concerted

pressure to critical points in the Confederacy. In the Virginia Theater the Shenandoah became the extended right flank of the Army of the Potomac. Grant hoped to use the Army of West Virginia to interdict and destroy that area's ability to supply Lee's army with needed materiel and foodstuffs. Neil, serving under Generals Franz Sigel, David Hunter, and Philip Sheridan, soon witnessed the bloody, fierce struggle, beginning with the Battle of New Market in May and ending with Sheridan's stunning victory at Cedar Creek on October 19, for control over the Valley.

The collapse of the Confederate presence in the Shenandoah in the fall of 1864 no longer necessitated the maintenance of a large Union army there. The greater need was in eastern Virginia. Grant then shifted Neil's regiment there in December 1864 to join the Army of the James and to participate in the final campaign against Lee. With the surrender of the Army of Northern Virginia at Appomattox five months later only one last assignment remained. Temporarily, Neil and the men of the 12th West Virginia served as part of the army of occupation in Richmond until June 1865.

At the war's end Neil was uncertain about his future. Considerable excitement gripped some in the army over the prospect of "emigrating" to Mexico. Even Neil considered "that 'tis very possible that I may join my fortunes with others who go."[7] But a more realistic possibility soon caught his attention. The prospect of a surgeon's commission in a "new consolidated Regiment" had a much greater appeal, and he believed that his chances were "very good."[8] However, on June 16 Neil, without a commission and along with his regiment, was mustered out of the army in Richmond. Returning to Wheeling in late June with his regiment, a pleased Neil wrote to his parents that they were to be accorded "a grand supper & oration given to my Regiment and the 15th Va., by the citizens." However, he cautioned them not to expect him to return home too soon. "We will not get away from here, perhaps, for about a week at which time you may look out for me."[9]

Returning shortly thereafter to Ohio, Neil initially established a medical practice at Sunbury. There he married Marietta Elliott, the daughter of D. H. Elliott, a large land owner, in September of the following year.[10] His military service as a regimental surgeon, as he well knew, provided him with an excellent background which would serve him well in his civilian career. Earlier in July 1864, in answer to a query from his parents about the possibility of resigning his commission, Neil replied that he "expect to stick it out to the last," for as he pointed out, "I have already . . . had more experience than some of the oldest practitioners in civil practice and particularly in the branch of operative surgery [I] have had a fine field of experience."[11] In 1867 apparently Neil went to London for a year to study British medical techniques and practices at St. Bartholomew Hospital and Guy's Hospital. Professionally ambitious and undoubtedly seeing the greater opportunities to be had in Columbus, he decided to move his practice there in 1870.

In the Ohio state capital Neil quickly became one of the city's most prominent physicians.[12] He became active and achieved increasing stature in Ohio medical circles. In January 1869 Neil, as a charter member, helped to organize the Central Ohio Medical Association and was elected to its board of censors. He also became a member of the American and Mississippi Valley Medical Associations. During the 1870s he served as a professor of surgery on the faculty of the College of Physicians and Surgeons in Columbus and contributed papers for publication in various medical journals. In 1878 he was elected to the presidency of the Columbus Academy of Medicine.[13] Reflective of his professional stature, he testified for the defense in the assassination trial of President James A. Garfield. He appeared, not as an expert on insanity, but to relate his one contact with Charles J. Guiteau and his impression of him.[14] Adding civic affairs to his professional life, Neil served on the Columbus school board from 1872 until 1890. Finally on February 14, 1901, after a long and distinguished career, Alexander Neil died of heart failure and dropsy.[15]

Neil left to posterity his wartime experiences in a series of letters which are in the Alderman Library of the University of Virginia and now with the Library's permission published for the first time. Neil loved to write, and it is obvious that in writing to his family and friends he saw his letters as a journal to be preserved by them for him. For the interest of the contemporary reader, the letters fortunately contain very little private family material; they deal primarily with military life and campaigns and his observations and impressions of those events in which he participated. Occasionally he indulged in literary license and hyperbole. More often, however, his letters form a vivid impression, with a humorous flair, of the Civil War through the eyes of an army surgeon.

Some judicious editing in preparing the letters for publication was used. A few editorial changes were made. The spelling of names and places was corrected, and punctuation, such as commas and semicolons, was substituted for dashes to aid the reader. On occasion missing periods and commas, where it seemed appropriate to supply one, were also added. Otherwise they remain as Dr. Alexander Neil wrote them, sometimes in haste and at other times in the leisure of camp.

Chapter I

"The Valley of Humiliation"
February 28–July 3, 1864

Alexander Neil, writing to his family in the aftermath of the Union's disastrous defeat at New Market, recounted what a local woman had prophesied as she watched the Federal army move up the Shenandoah Valley. Reflecting on previous probes into the region, she told Neil, "That we had a long and bloody road to travel, that disaster after disaster had always befallen our arms in this valley & would always continue so to do." Confronted by her after the battle, she asked, if "her prophecy had not been verified." Neil admitted, "I could not deny."[1] Indeed, Major General Franz Sigel's debacle was merely one in a series of reverses that had plagued Union forces. For two years the Shenandoah Valley had proven to be troublesome. Union soldiers dubbed it the "Valley of Humiliation." The Shenandoah, stretching some 170 miles northeastward from the James River to the Potomac River and bounded on the east by the Blue Ridge mountains and on the west by the Alleghenies, was strategically an important region for the Confederacy. Geographically, it provided a Southern army with an avenue of attack into the very heart of western Maryland and southern Pennsylvania. In the spring of 1862, Major General Thomas "Stonewall" Jackson had made himself and the Valley famous with his campaign to relieve pressure on Richmond by tying up two Federal armies attempting to capture him there. In the process he diverted Brigadier General Irwin McDowell's southward movement from Manassas to join General

1

George McClellan before Richmond. Adding insult to injury, Jackson—after striking at Major General John C. Fremont's and Major General Nathaniel Banks' armies—quickly slipped out of the Valley to join General Robert E. Lee in repulsing McClellan. The use of the Shenandoah in diverting pressure from the Confederate capital by threatening Maryland, Pennsylvania, and even Washington itself was not lost on the Southerners.

In September 1862, attention was again focused on the lower Valley. Lee, following his victory at the battle of Second Manassas, undertook a counter-offensive into western Maryland. The Army of Northern Virginia, moving up along the eastern slope of the Blue Ridge, fanned out into Maryland. Ultimately checked at Antietam by McClellan, the Confederate army retreated safely back through the Shenandoah. In the following summer, Lee took advantage of his stunning victory over General Joseph Hooker at Chancellorsville. He assumed the offensive and moved down the Valley. "Gobbling up" Brigadier General Robert Milroy's troops at Winchester, the Confederates crossed the Potomac River into the Cumberland Valley of western Maryland and struck into southern Pennsylvania. Badly repulsed at Gettysburg, the Army of Northern Virginia withdrew to the Rappahannock-Rapidan line to await the renewal of the campaign season in 1864.

Military considerations were not the Shenandoah's only significance. Agriculturally rich, the Valley was an important breadbasket for the Army of Northern Virginia. The fertile limestone-laced soil provided an abundance of wheat, corn, meat, and forage. Mills and granaries dotted the countryside. In addition local iron deposits provided ore for numerous forges. To the southwest, below where the Valley narrows and the James River passes through the Blue Ridge, the valley system resumes in an array of smaller ones stretching into Tennessee. In that area lay the important salt wells of the Saltville region and the lead mines around Wytheville, critical commodities for the Confederate war effort.

Linking those badly needed resources to the East were two rail lines and a canal. The Virginia and Tennessee Railroad, stretching from Bristol to Lynchburg, served to connect the Southwest, especially Saltville and Wytheville, with other railroads leading to Richmond. Further to the North ran the James River and Kanawha Canal running along the James River with its western terminus at Buchanan. Some twenty miles to the North a branch connected Lexington to the main artery. The canal tied them directly to Lynchburg and Richmond. Some thirty-six miles down the Valley the Virginia Central Railroad, running from Jackson's River depot to Staunton and then to Charlottesville and Gordonsville, linked the agriculturally rich

Harper's Ferry, West Virginia, circa 1862
Looking southwest into Harper's Ferry just after Stonewall Jackson's raid.

counties of the upper Shenandoah to Richmond by its connection
with the Orange and Alexandria Railroad.[2]

Union authorities realized the importance of those arteries to
the Confederacy in sustaining its war effort in Virginia. Federal success in that region would also allow the shift of additional troops
from there to eastern Virginia in order to augment the increasing
pressure on Richmond and force the abandonment of the Southern
capital. Such an accomplishment would be a devastating symbolic
and strategic blow to the Confederacy.

Efforts to cripple Lee's western support system had begun in
the summer of 1863. A Federal cavalry raid attempted to strike at
the Virginia and Tennessee Railroad two weeks after the battle of
Gettysburg but failed. Later, another expedition, originating from
Huntington, West Virginia, tried to reach the railroad and lead mines
but faltered at Wytheville. Finally, in December 1863 a more successful raid under Brigadier General William W. Averell managed to
reach the Virginia and Tennessee at Salem and briefly occupied that
town. Before withdrawing, Averell's men destroyed a quantity of
military supplies and inflicted considerable damage to the railroad
and depot.

However, Federal efforts to move up the Shenandoah Valley
towards Staunton remained unsuccessful. No Union army had ever
penetrated beyond the North River. Staunton, a major military supply center for the Confederacy on the Virginia Central Railroad and
less than thirty miles from Harrisonburg, remained safe and continued to defy capture. Union authorities, frustrated by their inability
to destroy these western transportation arteries and resources and
to control the Shenandoah Valley, placed a high priority on the area
in 1864. Success there, they believed, would play a key role in ending military operations in eastern Virginia and bring about the fall
of Richmond.

By the opening of the 1864 campaign, Federal authorities fully
intended to improve their fortune in the Valley, and the major change
in the Union command structure that spring radically enhanced their
chance of success. All armies and military operations were centrally
coordinated under the command of General Ulysses S. Grant, who
in the aftermath of his victories at Vicksburg and Lookout Mountain became general-in-chief of all the Northern armies. Under his
supervision, Federal armies applied concerted pressure on the Confederacy at various strategic points. In the Southwest Brigadier General William T. Sherman struck at General Joseph Johnston's army
in Georgia. In the eastern Virginia theatre Grant charged General

George Meade's Army of the Potomac with the objective of defeating Lee's Army of Northern Virginia; its surrender or destruction would mean the capture of Richmond. Striking at the Confederacy's two major armies simultaneously prevented the South from using interior lines to shift troops to defend threatened points.

In a subordinate role Major General Benjamin Butler and his Army of the James operated in concert with Meade. Butler, after taking City Point, was charged with moving up the south side of the James River, investing Richmond, and anchoring his left flank on the river above the city. If Meade forced Lee and his army back into the defenses of the city, then the two armies could unite and act as one.[3] Grant also intended to apply pressure in western Virginia. He proposed to use raids in that region to strike at Lee's support system of transportation and supplies in order to cripple his ability to wage war. Grant's integration of that area into the operations of eastern Virginia transformed western Virginia into Lee's extended left flank.

Initially, Major General Franz Sigel, commander of the Department of West Virginia, supervised operations in the Shenandoah Valley and southwestern Virginia. Sigel, unfortunately and for good reasons, enjoyed neither the full confidence of Washington nor the general-in-chief. Nonetheless, despite Grant's reservations, he confided to Sherman, "I do not calculate on very great results . . . if Sigel cant skin himself he can hold a leg whilest some one else skins."[4] Grant's strategy for western Virginia employed two pincer movements to penetrate the region. A column of infantry under Brigadier General George Crook, moving from Gauley Bridge, West Virginia, drove towards the Tennessee and Virginia Railroad's bridge over the New River and destroyed it and large segments of the rail line. Crook's cavalry under Averell, moving on a different route, struck at Wytheville and Saltville in an attempt to destroy the lead mines and salt works there. Unsuccessful, they rejoined the main army under Crook. Originally, if their operations were successful, they were either to continue destroying the railroad towards Lynchburg or to turn north and connect with Sigel. Instead, Crook withdrew into West Virginia. The second column, under the direct command of Sigel, advanced up the Shenandoah Valley towards Staunton. Grant hoped that Sigel's army could capture and destroy the important military and railroad depot there.

In late April Sigel began concentrating Crook's army at Gauley Bridge and his column at Martinsburg. Finally on April 28th he was ready and wired Grant that he would "move to-morrow to Bunker Hill."[5] With considerable fanfare his column left Martinsburg on the following day. Stopping only briefly at Bunker Hill, Sigel reached

Winchester on May 1st. There the general became increasingly cautious. The day after his arrival he telegraphed Grant that "I am to occupy the line at Cedar Creek and to advance up the Shenandoah valley if present circumstances will allow me to do so. To advance beyond Strasburg with my present force is hardly possible. . . ."[6] He would remain at Winchester until May 9. Yet, he was confident that Brigadier General John Imboden's Valley forces were not that sizeable. He estimated them at approximately 3,000 infantry and cavalry.[7]

His march to Cedar Creek proved uneventful. There he was joined by Brigadier Jeremiah Cutler Sullivan's infantry division. Probing further south, his army reached Woodstock on May 11. Encountering resistance from Confederate units, his cavalry quickly drove them back towards Edinburg. At Woodstock Sigel's men luckily captured important dispatches which divulged Confederate deployments and movements in the upper Valley. They disclosed the movement of Major General John C. Breckinridge's army towards Staunton. The dispatches also revealed Confederate anxiety over the possibility of Sigel's force moving across the Blue Ridge towards Charlottesville to join Grant. The Federal commander would later write that it "could not fail to prompt me to energetic action." Yet, in a wire on May 13 to the adjutant general he indicated that "My forces are insufficient for offensive operations in this county. . . . My intention, therefore is not to advance farther than this place with my main force, but have sent out strong parties in every direction."[8]

Those parties were to move towards New Market, some twenty miles up the Valley. Sigel took note of the town's strategic position. There an important artery connecting the Allegheny region beyond Brock's Gap crossed the Valley Pike and headed east across Massanutten Gap into Page Valley and then through Thorton's Gap into the Virginia Piedmont. An advance unit controlling that point would sharpen Confederate fears that the Federals might indeed move east to join Grant.[9] Anxious to determine Confederate strength in the area, despite the risk of dividing his army, Sigel decided to send a cavalry probe towards the town. Major General Julius Stahel, commander of the 1st Cavalry Division, chose Colonel Augustus Moor of the 1st Brigade, 1st Infantry Division, to lead the reconnaissance expedition, consisting of three regiments, a battery, and a thousand cavalry. David Hunter Strother, a member of Sigel's staff, concerned about two other cavalry detachments that Sigel had made, worried that in pushing Moor's brigade so far in advance, the Confederates might destroy the army in detail.[10]

Once Moor's men reached Mount Jackson, they encountered increasing opposition from Imboden's forces. Skirmishing with Confederates at Rude's Hill, the Federals drove them back to the edge of New Market. Sigel, receiving reports of the fight, did not believe that they indicated a sizable Southern force and decided to continue his advance towards the town. However, Major Theodore F. Lang of his staff, conducting a reconnaissance for the general, reported that Breckinridge had joined Imboden and that they were about to attack Moor. He further suggested to Sigel that he should bring up his entire command quickly. Lacking an immediate response to his despatches, an exasperated Lang told Sigel "that he must bring up his entire force . . . and to come at once, otherwise he would be too late."[11] Forced to be decisive, Sigel, believing that a retreat would psychologically have an adverse impact on his army and that controlling the important crossroads at New Market would be strategically important, pressed on. The general's estimate of Breckinridge's strength also shaped his decision. Sigel believed that it would be approximately equal to his own; unfortunately for him, he erroneously assumed that Breckinridge's men would not all be up yet. That belief, coupled with Moor's success on the previous day, fortified Sigel's assumption that if a battle did develop, his chances of victory were good. He, therefore, resolved to hold Imboden's forces in check until he could bring up his main army and "then accept battle."[12] However, the decision demanded immediate action. He did not have the luxury of leisurely concentrating his army. Parts of his army remained strung out along the Valley Pike and never saw action. With Breckinridge ready to give battle, Sigel's decision proved disastrous.

Sigel's defeat merely confirmed the suspicions and opinions of the authorities in Washington. Halleck sarcastically telegraphed Grant that "Instead of advancing on Staunton he is already in full retreat on Strasburg. If you expect anything from him you will be mistaken. He will do nothing but run. He never did anything else."[13] The War Department quickly prepared to replace him. Within four days Major General David Hunter, with the concurrence of Grant, was assigned to the command. Hunter, a professional soldier but one with better political skills than military ones, would soon earn the hatred of Virginians. A landscape of destruction, burnt homes and public buildings, and the sting of vindictiveness symbolized for them the epitome of villainy and infamy. The *Richmond Whig* dubbed him, "Hunter, the Hyena."[14]

Hunter quickly assumed command and reorganized the army. Determined to renew active campaigning, Hunter sent orders to Crook and Averell to move on Staunton. Reinforcing his objective, instructions from Grant underscored that goal for his army.[15] Hunter, initially concerned that Breckinridge had been reinforced, feared increasing Confederate strength could easily block any movement farther south. David Strother, reflecting this opinion, recorded in his diary, "It looks therefore as if we could do no more than demonstrations. We cannot go safely beyond Mr. Jackson. . . ."[16] That factor, however, quickly disappeared. Lee, hard pressed by Meade, needed Breckinridge's men and ordered him to join the Army of Northern Virginia. Breckinridge's removal left a weak, variegated array of Southern forces, ranging from Imboden's men to local militia units to defend the upper Valley. Informed of that development and no longer facing a formidable opponent, Hunter's army began its move on Staunton on May 26.

Imboden's force, far too small, could offer only delaying resistance. In desperation he wired Lee that there was no point south of Mount Crawford "where I can successfully resist him, and there it is very doubtful, though I will do my best."[17] Hunter's army, briefly delayed in Woodstock to be refitted with shoes, soon occupied New Market. Pushing through Harrisonburg, Hunter received reports that the Confederates, under the command of Brigadier General William "Grumble" Jones,[18] were concentrating along the North River.

Shrewdly, Hunter decided against a frontal attack on the Confederate line's strong positions. Instead, upon leaving Harrisonburg, Hunter marched his men in an extended left flanking movement down the Port Republic road to bypass Jones. Surprised, the Confederates quickly moved to block his advance. At the little village of Piedmont, Jones prepared to give battle. Despite objections from Imboden, Jones chose a strong position. However, in the deployment of his army he allowed a fatal gap to exist between the infantry and cavalry. Capitalizing on that flaw, Hunter achieved a stunning Union victory: Jones was killed and his army shattered. The long sought goal of capturing Staunton was finally within the Union's grasp.

It was at Staunton that Hunter made his fateful decision to strike at Lynchburg. Earlier Grant on May 26 had indicated that he should "push on if possible to Charlottesville and Lynchburg. . . ."[19] Initially Hunter's staff opposed it, but a decision was postponed until the arrival of Crook's Army of the Kanawha. Once the juncture of the two armies was accomplished, a proposal by Averell of continuing to move up the Valley and then turning east over the Peaks of Otter to attack Lynchburg was adopted. Averell's plan, in contrast to Grant's, called for a more extended and militarily circuitous route. The proposal had its critics. Crook put forth serious reservations. In a conversation with Strother he warned that "if we expected to take Lynchburg at all we must move upon it immediately and rapidly." Hunter's reply was "that a good deal of delay was unavoidable."[20] Sadly, the general's acceptance of that premise proved to be nearly fatal. United, the Army of West Virginia, some 20,000 strong, was a formidable army in western Virginia. Soon Lexington, the home of Virginia Military Institute, and Buchanan, the western terminus of the James River and Kanawha Canal, experienced their first tastes of war. Crossing the Peaks of Otter, the army by mid-June cautiously approached Lynchburg. No other Federal army had ever penetrated that deeply into the Virginia heartland. By the evening of June 17 Federal units were skirmishing with Southerners within less than five miles of the city.

After that premise of that premise proved to be nearly fatal. Although he was hard pressed by Grant, Lee could hardly afford to allow Lynchburg, an important supply and rail center, to fall to a Federal army. The city, lightly defended, was extremely vulnerable. Recognizing that fact, Lee detached General Jubal Early's troops to rush to its defense. Early's movements, in contrast to those of Hunter's, were swift and effective. Confederate reinforcements began arriving as the Federals commenced probing the city's outer defenses. Hunter's boldness gave way to anxiety. Southern reinforcements, Early's cleverness in projecting an image of a superior army —despite its reality—and the growing Federal shortage of ammunition and commissariat supplies quickly fed Hunter's fears of an impending disaster. Safety for his army suddenly became the general's primary concern. In a meeting with his commanders on the afternoon of June 18 Hunter decided on withdrawal.[21]

After a day of probing and skirmishing, the Army of West Virginia under the cover of darkness quietly moved back down the Bedford turnpike towards Liberty and West Virginia. An unrelenting Confederate pursuit constantly threatened their arduous and hurried retreat. Hunter's army had to pass Salem and continue into the mountains before the Federals felt fully secure from Early. However, deprivations proved to be a more serious enemy than the Confederates. Severe shortages of food caused serious suffering until June 27 when a supply train with desperately needed rations reached the army near Gauley Bridge. The Army of West Virginia, wearied, half-starved, and exhausted, badly needed a respite. Army morale was low, and its men required rest and refitting. For two days the army rested at Gauley Bridge before Hunter continued on to Charleston. Not until mid-July did Hunter's army return to western Maryland and the lower Valley to resume campaigning.

1

Cumberland, Maryland
Sunday morning 7 oclock February 28, 1864

Dear Father & Mother,

Your last letter was received in due time and I now proceed
to answer, this beautiful Sabbath morning, before breakfast, so
that I will get time to attend Church this forenoon and sunday
school this afternoon, also Church this evening. Since I last wrote
you, there has nothing very unusual transpired in this Department. Feby 22, Washington's Birth Day was celebrated here in a
becoming manner by firing of cannon and a general review of
the troops here by Genl. Kelley[22]; everything passing off smoothly.

I believe it is officially announced that Genl. Sigel has superseded Genl. Kelley in Command of this Department and will be
here in a day or two.[23] Then we will pass from under the fatherly
care of Genl. Kelley, who has always treated us kindly, to "*fight
mit Sigel*" and his lager beer and sour crouk sattelites [*sic*], but I
sincerely hope it may be for the better as there have been so
many complaints here that our forces in this Department have
been almost as inefficient for the protection of the country as if
we had no army on foot in this quarter. All along the Potomac
and all along the Baltimore & Ohio Rail Road there is a feeling of
uncertainty and insecurity which ought not to exist. Genl. Kelley
has an army of thirty five thousand men and should be able to
keep the country in perfect peace for the whole distance to Ohio.
Yet the enemy is continually harassing the inhabitants of this
region, plundering our military stations and from time to time
tearing up the railroad, burning the bridges and interrupting a
communication which should be permanently undisturbed. It is
complained here that Genl. Kelley allows the Rebels to escape
when he might overtake and defeat them; that he guards negli-
gently our wagon trains and stores, suffering them to fall into
the hands of the enemy; that he allows false dispatches from his
subordinates to be sent to the Government and published in the
newspapers, claiming victories that are never won and subsequently takes no pains to correct them. So successful has the
enemy been in obtaining possession of our stores that Genl. Kelley
has been called in this quarter, the Rebel Quartermaster. In the
capture of the various wagon trains between New Creek and
Petersburg,[24] it is estimated that the Government has lost a million of dollars, besides a considerable number of men, to say
nothing of the moral affect of such disasters. And yet after all

this, it is said that the Genl. is as brave, active, resolute and sagacious an officer as there is in the service and that he has only been unfortunate.

How true this all may be I am unable to judge, only I give you the unvarnished facts as near as I can gather from the military gossiping that I hear every day, but I really hope that Genl. Sigel has been born under a more lucky star and may give better satisfaction. Say nothing about this as it is contrary to Regulations for officers to talk either favorably or unfavorably of their Superiors and the Genl. has always treated me courteously and I know has done well by our Regiment. The boys are afraid when Sigel comes that we will be removed to the Rapidan or perhaps South and our place filled here by Sagen beer dutchman. I hope this may not be.

I herewith enclose you photographs of Daniel Giffin, Alex Gilmore, and Lieutenants Burley & Whittingham. I want you to preserve carefully all the photographs I send you and after next pay day I will send you an album in which to put them. All our officers are getting up albums of their brother officers, which will be nice things to look at in years to come. But the breakfast bell is ringing and odors of frying beef steak and boiling coffee come welcome to my nose and I must stop writing, hoping to hear from you soon & often.

Yours Truly

Alex.

2

Cumberland, Maryland
Saturday Eve. March 5, 1864

Dear Father & Mother,

I recd. your last letter some few days since and was very glad to hear from you, but sorry that you complain of that difficulty about your face. It seems to be of an erysipelatous nature, from the description you give of it, and if so, you will probably obtain relief from the remedies which I enclose a prescription for and which you can procure at the drug store for a trifle. You can continue the use of them for a few days, at least.

You enclosed, in your last, an obituary of Frank Woods who was killed at Chickamauga. I was very intimately acquainted with him for a number of years at Delaware and learned of his death whilst at home this winter. He was a splendid boy.

We were mustered for pay on last Monday, but the Paymaster writes us that he has no money and does not know when he will get any. So it may be some length of time before we are paid again.

I recd. a letter from John a day or two since which I answered to-day.

There has nothing new occurred in this Department since my last. Sigel has not arrived yet, but will come next Monday, I understand.

The weather is mild and balmy, and every thing augurs an early Spring. Hoping to hear from you soon I close by enclosing photographs of Major Brown, Capt. Bristor & Lieutenants Brenneman and Pigott, also Charlie Odbert Hospital Steaward, which take good care of.[25]

Your Truly

Alex.

3

Cumberland, Maryland
Saturday night March 12, 1864

Dear Father & Mother,

I received your last letter dated the 7th inst. in due time and now hasten to reply.

I am very sorry that your health is so very poor and hope that you may recover soon, as it is hard to be so afflicted. My health still continues very good with the exception of a very bad cold at present.

Genl. Sigel & Staff arrived here last evening at 11 'oclock and was saluted by thirteen guns being fired at the depot. He assumed command to-day. When Genl. Kelley goes I am unable to state, the latter looks pale and melancholy.[26]

One of our Regiment was shot by a citizen, the other evening, in a street broil. He was shot in the head, though I think he may yet recover.

You say that Miss Ella Mercer, my old colleague, called on you. I should be pleased to see Miss Ella, as she is a very nice lady. I had never heard anything about her whereabouts since we left Centerville.

I chartered one of my ambulances, on last Tuesday, filled it with ladies and took an excursion to Frostburg, some ten miles distant, on the very summit of the Allegheny Mountains, staid till evening and had a very pleasant trip, as the day was lovely.

You ask about my boy George. I discharged him some six weeks since, for worthlessness, and procured him a good home, in the city with a citizen physician, where he still remains. I then employed another black boy Edward who had been a former servant of President Davis at Richmond, but he, proving to be of no account, I also discharged him, after which he enlisted in a Colored Regiment and has shouldered his musket and gone to the wars.

I now have a white man to take care of my horses & c. and henceforth will have nothing to do with the nigger.

I received the Advocate and Gazette the other day.

I herewith enclose photographs of Capt. Roberts, Lieutenants Means and Pierpont (nephew Governor Pierpont), also David Griffin our Sutler, all of which you will carefully preserve for me.[27] The evening is most delightful, very warm, and the moon is shinning.

You have doubtless read of poor Young Col. Dahlgren's brilliant dash on to Richmond and his unfortunate death. What a brave boy, to be thus buried like a dog.[28]

Hoping to hear from you soon & often I remain,

Yours Sincerely

Alex.

4

Cumberland, Maryland
Saturday Evening March 19, 1864

Dear Father and Mother,

Your letter of the 14th inst. was recd. by me on the morning of the 16th. I am glad to learn that mother's health is improving and hope she may get entirely well before long.

I recd. a letter from John[29] stating that Sattie had been quite sick but was getting better and that he expected to move the last of this month.

You mistake, in stating that Smiley is a sister's son of Geo. Atkinson. It is the Captain's wife who is the sister's daughter. He is of a different breed of "dogs."

I am glad to hear of Bunyan Wigton's marriage and that he has not forgotten us. If I knew where he is, I would write him a letter.

Major Brown is from Hancock Co., W.Va. in the panhandle. I will ask him, who his father was and learn his pedigree.

I was serenaded the other evening by a string band from Co. D. in which Daniel Maxwell was principal musician; there were also, Waddle, Blaney, and some other good singers and fiddlers, all from your old stomping grounds.

Our Lieut. Col. Northcott[30] of our Regiment passed through here this morning for his home in Clarksburg Va. He has just been released from the loathsome cells of Libby Prison Richmond where he has been confined since the middle of last June, having been taken prisoner at the battle of Winchester.[31]

He is said to be a man of very fine talents, and about the time the war began, was a refugee from Chattanooga, Tennessee at which place he edited a paper for many years. He is beloved by all with whom he is acquainted and will be joyfully welcomed back to our old Regiment.

Sigel was up to Camp to-day and inspected our new fort which is being built. He looks like a dried up, hard student and I have no doubt but that he is a very smart man.

Genl. Kelley is now absent on leave, to recruit his health which is very delicate.

No Paymaster yet. I was a bankrupt more than two weeks ago and was obliged to borrow money. I guess he will be along before many days. I should love to once more behold the radiance of his countenance.

I have not much news to write and write this Saturday evening in order to go to Church tomorrow. I attend the M.E. Church, which is a very fine large Church with an excellent pastor, Bro. Sears.[32] He has just returned from Conference, been returned the second year. He is a very loyal man and expresses himself quite freely in the pulpit, though a large portion of his congregation & members are secessionists. Last Sunday he finished his sermon by remarking that "Fifty years hence, sixty millions of American people would place the name of Abraham Lincoln, high up on the scroll of fame, at the side of the manes of Cromwell and Washington." He speaks out boldly, and I love him for it.

Hoping to hear from you soon I am,

Yours Truly

Alex.

5

Hd. Qrs. Dept. West Virginia
Cumberland, Md.
Friday Evening Mch 25, 1864

Dear Father & Mother,

Your last letter was recd. Wednesday morning, also two newspapers the next day.

I have nothing much to write that would interest you, as nothing very strange hereabouts happens these times.

The rebels still, however, make occasional raids in the neighborhood, the last of which, the other day, below here near the railroad, resulted in the capture by them of two members of the West Va. General Assembly, that were home on a visit. They were carried away to Richmond, though we sent a large cavalry force in pursuit, but did not, however, succeed in doing much. Sigel is reorganizing the whole Department and is getting very strict about every thing, using, by the way, a great deal of "red tape."

I should have been pleased to see Uncle Alec. I hope he may enjoy his visit and that you may use him well. Give him my kind regards.

I shall write to Dr. Riddle[33] before a great while I think, also to Aunt Miles people.

No Paymaster yet and the whole Regiment is bankrupt, myself included, having borrowed till I can borrow no more. I am now on the eve of a financial ruin as expenses are heavy.

I pay 4.$ per week for board which is the best I have done or can do; have broke the last X which is reduced to less than 7; the latter being the last remnant of a borrowed 20, and am in debt some to the Sutler, besides—not much. You know not the expenses of an army officer, the incidentals, the et-ceteras, hardly a week elapsing but I must contribute from 1 to 5.$ to send boxes of provisions to our prisoners in Richmond, and run to death in other gratuitous enterprises &c, &c.

I wish you would enclose me $10- in your next letter, and oblige me much, but say nothing about it to any one.

I enclose you photographs of Capt. Pritchard, Lt. Peirson, and Quartermaster Sergeant Fleming, all of 12 Va., also Lt. Quier 54 Pa., Lt. Schoff 15th Va. and Capt Melvin, Asst. Adjt. General Kelley's staff, all intimate friends of mine, which you will carefully preserve.

'Tis snowing very hard & the wind blows very cold, but I am in a good warm room with a good coal fire & enjoy myself finely.

I wish you would write as soon as you receive this.

Yours Truly,

Alex.

6

Cumberland, Md.
April 2, 1864

Dear Father & Mother,

Your letters mailed the 28th & 30th ult. are both recd. the last of which on Friday morning enclosing for me 10$, for which I thank you very much.

There has been a war council of four Major Generals here for the past day or two, the result of which is, we have marching orders for tomorrow morning, to go by rail somewhere, do not know where. I suspect the Spring Campaign has commenced and there will be a simultaneous movement of Sigels army with that of Grant's. I had made Calculations on staying here all summer, but how very uncertain every thing is in the army.

I have just this moment recd. a letter from Dr. Riddle asst. Surg. of the 61st Pa. Vols. in reply to one I wrote him a few days since. I send you his photograph which he sent me. He would like to hear from you all, also from his father. He sends you and John his best love. He is in the Grand Army of the Potomac and likes it much.

I will write you soon again.

Goodbye

Alex.

7

Philippi House
Tuesday Philippi, Va.
Evening
April 5, 1864

Dear Father & Mother,

I embrace this opportunity of dropping you a line, informing you that I am still alive. We arrived here about 5 P.M. this evening, marching from Webster since morning, over the worst roads and through the deepest mortar I ever saw, a great portion of the time we could only see, as the wagon train passed, the mules ears sticking from beneath the mud.

We left all of our baggage and camp equipage behind at Webster, under guard, and are marching without tents or any cover, our destination for the present, is Beverly Va. where we are to form a junction with another extensive force, then make a raid, somewhere, 'tis contraband for me to say.

You can watch the papers closely and know something before many days. It is a terrible thing on the soldiers, as it rains and snows all the time, and many fall by the way.

Phillippi is a pretty little town & the County seat of Barbour County. It is the memorable spot where the first engagement of the war took place, in May '61, in which Genl. Kelley was wounded, and the rebels routed.[34]

We are in a Brigade of Virginia Regiments, composed of the best fighting material of the army, and commanded by Col. Thoburn 1st Va. Regt. Our Division is to be commanded, I believe, by Major Genl. Ord.[35]

We left Cumberland on Sunday forenoon and arrived in Grafton about 10 that night, passed through the mountains where the snow was two feet deep. Changed cars in Grafton and arrived in Webster soon after, where we staid until this morning.

You may not hear again from me very soon, but do not be uneasy.

Excuse Haste

Goodbye

Alex.

8

Beverly Randolph Co. Va.
Friday Eve. Apr. 8, '64

Dear Father & Mother,

I wrote you last from Philippi, on the march. I again write you a line from this town at which we arrived last evening. After leaving Philippi the morning of the 6th we marched that day as far as the foot of Laurel Mountain, and encamped, not far from Garrick's ford, the memorable spot at which Genl. Garnett the rebel Genl. was killed, the summer of 1861, our forces at that time being commanded by Genl. Hill, who was subsequently Adjutant General of Ohio.[36] The next days march brought us to Beverly the County seat of Randolph Co. where we have lay [*sic*] Since. We are near Rich mountain and in sight of the old battle ground.

The roads are in such a condition that it seems almost impracticable for the artillery and wagons to get along.

For some reason, unknown, we are ordered tonight to be in readiness in the morning to start back to Webster.

The weather today was sunshiny & spring-like, but the snow in the mountains near, is from 3 to 5 feet deep.

We found here the 28th Ohio, & 10th & 11th Va., the first two Regiments having been here for the past 9 months.

They are very nicely fixed up.

This is a very miserably antiquated town of about 300 souls, mostly secessionists.

As the Colonel has just called at my room and desires me to call at his house and participate in some musical exercises with some ladies, I must close.

Yours Truly

Alex.

9

Philippi, Virginia
April 12, 1864

Dear Father & Mother,

By the above heading you will see that I am back at the old place again; arrived here yesterday about noon. I am left here with Major Brown and a detachment of our Regiment, the rest started on this morning for Webster. The Major is in command of the post and I am in charge of the sick. I will establish a Post Hospital today.

We are boarding at a very pleasant private house (the county Recorder's) right on the bank of the Tigress Valley River, have plenty of good piano music and every thing very cheerful within, though it rains & snows almost incessantly.

I wrote you from Beverly, since which we have had some terrible marching. Indeed, my horse is about give out, but will now get some rest, for a while at least.

My money is about "played out" though I borrowed some, since I recd yours.

It costs more on a march than at any other time, so I wish you would in your next, send me another 10.$. The letter will follow me without fail, should I move from this point.

I have not recd. your last letter, but will soon I have no doubt.

Tell John that I will write to him soon, & let me know his Postoffice Address. Tell him I saw the Adjutant General of W.Va.

who called on me at Cumberland and learn from him that they will make no more appointments of Ohio men, as they have done more now for Ohio men, than the troops, furnished by Ohio from Virginia Regiments, will justify.

I have nothing further to add, I believe, and will hurry & mail my letter.

Address me

Philippi W.Va.

Yours Truly

Alex.

I send you curl from the head of a little rebel girl.

10

Philippi, W.Va.
Sunday April 17, 1864

Dear Father & Mother,

I recd. your partnership letter the other day and was glad to hear from you all. I had written you a day or two previous; have written you several letters in the last two weeks. I am still at Philippi, and being the only medical officer present and Post Surgeon, am having very pleasant times, and in all probability will remain here sometime until the roads get passable for our artillery and wagon train. Then we will move with a heavy force on to Staunton. We will have a good deal of hard fighting to do on the route as the rebels now are fortifying Cheat Mountain & will hotly contest our passage I have no doubt. The bad & stormy weather has materially changed our original programme.

I recd. a letter from cousin Lynes Miles the other day, also one from Minnie Richards. I wrote to them to day, also to Dr. Riddle.

I recd. two papers from home the other day. Your last letter recd. was dated April 7.

Write soon

Philippi W.Va.

Alex.

11

Martinsburg, Va.[37]
April 23, 1864

My Dear Friends,

After travelling hundreds of miles by rail and by road, we are again back at sweet old Martinsburg, in which I set my foot, first nearly nine months ago. On our arrival last night we were hailed with the greatest delight by our old friends.

We passed through Cumberland Md. yesterday about noon, stopping there about one hour. As we came in the city, we were welcomed with beautiful music, many cheers and a thousand handkerchiefs fluttered in the breeze from as many white hands.

I staid at Philippi nine days & enjoyed it very much and on the eve of the 20th left that place, marching on the night to Webster where we were joined next evening with our other detachment, marched to Grafton, and embarked for this point where we arrived last night about 9 P.M.

We are concentrating a force here, to go up the Valley. I think our Brigade is all busted up, and the original programme materially changed.

I have recd. no letter from you since the one dated the 7th inst. but am confident that all letters you have written will follow me.

I wrote for more money in one of my letters from Philippi; this I am anxious to receive as I am broke. We will see no paymaster until next month. Then will receive four months pay. I may have to draw occasionally on you before that time.

It is warm as summer time. How different from the weather in the mountains about Beverly.

I am hurried,

Write soon to

Martinsburg

Va.

12

Hospital 2nd Brigade 1st Division
Martinsburg, Va.
April 28, 64

Dear Father & Mother,

I am this moment in receipt of your letter enclosing the X, for which I am much obliged.

One week ago, to-day, I was, by order of the Medical Director, put in charge of our Brigade Hospital, occupying the Presbyterian Church for that purpose, and a room in the Court House for a Dispensary & office.

Our forces have marching orders for the morning at 5 oclock. I suppose up the old Valley again.

I have not learned whether I shall be relieved here or not, but think it is very probable I shall accompany my Regiment.

Sigel is here himself, also Maj. Genl Stahel and Brig. Genls. Sullivan and Weber, Sullivan commanding our division.[38]

The hills and valleys are fairly covered with camps and the town is flooded with hundreds of officers from Major Genls. down, and reinforcements are constantly coming in.

I have heard Sigel make several speeches in response to Serenading Bands.

He makes no boast, but says that he hopes this campaign will end the war. He compliments our West Virginia troops very highly.

We had a grand review on yesterday, lasting several hours, near town.

Our line of Battle extended about 5 miles, and in the fluttering of a hundred banners, the gleaming of bayonets, the flashing of sabers, and on "all the pomp and circumstance of war," the bright April sun shone down clear and beautiful, the booming of cannon and the sweet strains of music from a score of bands, lending additional enchantment to the scene, rendering it magnificent beyond description. As Genls. Sigel & Stahel with their respective staffs & orderlies rode up and down the lines the heavens were almost rent with cheers.

I had a large field glass and from my position, could see almost every thing that transpired. I lent my horse to another staff officer and went in an ambulance, accompanied by some ladies, amongst whom was Miss Jane Boswell Moore of Baltimore,[39] who is visiting this place at present. You have doubtless read of her often. She is beautiful young lady of about 19 years of age & of considerable personal attraction; is of great means & influence; and has, ever, since the war began, devoted her whole time and energies towards alleviating the sufferings of our soldiers. She has during that time, as an agent for the Sanitary & Christian Commissions, visited nearly all the camps & battlefields of our army, frequently admist the din of battle, exposed to the heaviest fire of the enemy, & many times destitute of any thing to eat for two days at a time. She has written a very neat & elegant work entitled "Scenes on the Potomac" which has been read by most every one. On arriving here, she made me a visit, and I took an ambulance and accompanied her through the different camps, helping her distribute books & papers to our needy soldiers. As we were coming off the field yesterday from the Review, in our carriage, Maj. Genl. Sigel espied her, sitting by my side, looking through my Glass, & recognizing her in a moment he galloped up & very cordially shook her hand, introducing at the time Maj. Genl Stahel. All the Generals of our army are her warm friends & gladly welcome her. I have promised her, to go this afternoon with her to Sigel's Headquarters to have a private conference with the Genl. relative to her mission.

Since writing the above, I have received an order from Hd.qr. detailing me to establish a Post Hospital at this place for the whole Division & take exclusive charge of the same. I very gladly welcome the order.

I must immediately go to work to organize my Hospital Department & get things in raming order, which is a big thing.[40]

Good Bye. The weather is lovely.

Address me

At Martinsburg Va.

Alex.

Evening

P.S. Since writing my letter I have recd. another order relieving me from taking charge of Post Hospital & to report to my Regiment.

It seems that after I had been detailed, an old dilapidated Surgeon of an Ohio Regiment, claiming to be out of health and unable to make a journey, went to the Medical Director and begged him to have him detailed, and as I was able bodied & stout, he succeeded in, superseding me & hence I was relieved. The boys are glad as they want me along in the field. So off to the wars I go on the morning with the forces.

I was a little sorry but I suppose it is all right.

You may address me as usual to Martinsburg & all communications will follow me.

I am Yours Truly

Alex.

13

Sigel's Grand Army on the March
Camp at Bunker Hill[41]
April 30th, 1864

Dear Father & Mother,

Your last letter dated 27th inst. containing another remittance of a greenback, reached me last evening on the march. We left Martinsburg yesterday morning, reaching this place in the evening. I think we will remain here to-day, as it is muster-for pay-day, then we will move up the valley, to act in junction with Meade's army.

Our army presents a very imposing appearance, with Genl. Sigel riding at its head, accompanied with Genls. Stahel, chief of cavalry & Sullivan, commanding the infantry, our column over six miles in length & requiring over 2 hours to pass a fixed point. (This is contraband).

The pike is most elegant to travel on and the weather salubrious and sunshiny, but the evenings quite cold. Our couch is the green sward of nature and our covering the broad canopy of heaven.

Vegetation is getting much luxuriant, the flowers are blooming & the trees full of blossoms, and the grass makes excellent pasture for our horses.

Everybody is in good spirits and confident of a successful campaign. The camp is enliven by the music from numerous brass bands which are discoursing sweet music and rendering every thing cheerful.

The evening before we left Martinsburg, I called on the French Minister's Lady & Family; (Mrs. Faulkner) she was very glad to see me, & still claims to be a staunch Union woman. She still lives in the most elegant style. Her husband Hon. Chas J. is yet in the Confederate Army, also two sons who are battling for their "sacred rights."[42]

I must close as a courier goes back with mail matter.

Yours Truly

Alex

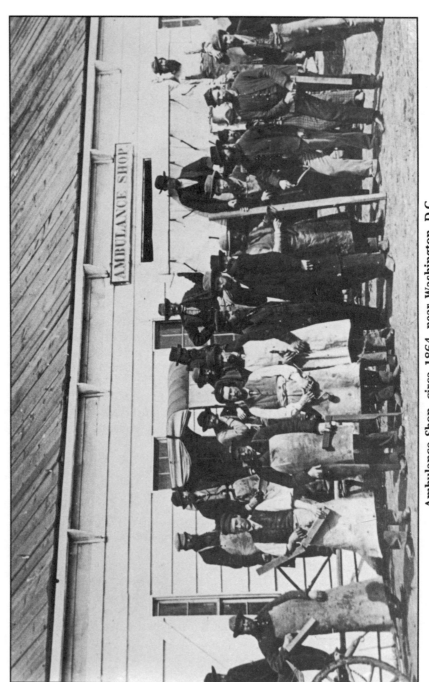

Ambulance Shop, circa 1864, near Washington, D.C.

14

Winchester, Va.[43] *Thursday*
May 5, 1864

Dear Father & Mother,

I recd. one of your Philippi letters today & now hasten to reply.

We arrived here Sunday Evening May 1st, where we have been encamped since, but are ready to move at any moment; the weather is most delightful and every body confident of a successful campaign; we are getting reinforcements daily & now have a very respectable army; so state our Commanders & our number is Contraband, but you will hear from us before many days in the papers, though every thing is kept remarkably still at present.

I wrote you from Bunker Hill which place we left Sunday morning.

This is the Garden spot of the "old dominion" where the F.F.V.'s[44] once flourished under their own vine and fig tree, where the homes are of the brave chivalry and "defenders of homes and firesides" now away battling for "Southern Rights."

Winchester was once the most beautiful city of Virginia, with her shaded avenues, princely mansions and handsome flower-gardens, the home of the aristocratic and wealthy. But now one thinks of an eternal Sunday, as he wanders through her lonely streets and beholds ruined walls. Tenantless houses, demolished churches, and in the outskirts, desecrated cemeteries, in which are the shattered remnants of costly monuments, rent to pieces by shot and shell in the many sanguinary struggles enacted here during the past three years. Many brave soldiers have been buried here, Union & Secesh. Each with a little white head-board to mark the spot.

From among the many rebel epitaphs here I selected some for my journal, among which are the following.

Lt. Sidney Wannamaker Co. H. 3rd Regt. S.C. Vols. age 28 yrs.

"What though we die upon the field
'I will from that never will we yield
'Twill show the foe that like a flood
We pour for southern rights our blood."
                on another the following:
"Yes they who for their Country die
Shall fill an honored grave
While glory lights the soldier's tomb
And beauty weeps the brave"

Another

"Here lies a soldier of Christ and of the Confederacy"

A few thousand people still inhabit this once pretty city, but among these only a very few righteous, and these with the "rebs" have been brought almost to the verge of starvation, a blockade on either side shutting them from and isolating them from the outerworld, & depriving them from the very necessaries of life. I have formed the acquaintance of some Union families who have suffered every thing from this miserable Southern Rights doctrine.

I have been cordially welcome at the house of a Secessionist, the wealthiest man in the county, whose son I so befriended last winter whilst a prisoner in our hands up the valley. They live in the most magnificent style and are very kind people.

We are encamped about a mile from town on the battlefield where many brave boys of my Regiment fell that 13, 14 & 15th June last year, under the brave Milroy. We find some of their bones bleaching in the sunshine.

I understand that the Rebels attacked Martinsburg last night. I did not learn the result. They captured a wagon train night before last on its way from Martinsburg to this place with supplies.[45] Our provisions are cut pretty short & many a meal I have made on a hard cracker & some coffee, but still my health continues very good, & my faith is strong that this campaign will end the war and never will I leave the field until that is accomplished, if any life is preserved. I will try & send this back with an officer to Martinsburg to mail. You will address me Via Martinsburg Va. & your letters will follow me.

15

Camp near Winchester Va.
Sunday Afternoon May 8, '64

Dear Father & Mother,

One week ago this evening we arrived here and encamped on these broad plains & beautiful hills, our camp extending for miles, with clear springs of water and many living streams of the same intervening, rendering it beautiful & cheerful for the soldier, though our crackers are "cut very short" some of the time and we are on very low diet.

I wrote to you twice since arriving here, but do not receive many letters as our mail privileges are some what restricted and we have to watch opportunities to run our letters through by private couriers.

Miss Jane Boswell Moore of whom I have spoken has just arrived on her mission of mercy & says she will take a letter back to Martinsburg in the morning. I am informed that we move in the morning on up the valley and I suppose this will be my last opportunity of writing to you & therefore I scratch you a line on my knee to let you know that I am well, also to advise you that you need not get uneasy should you not hear from me again very soon.

Our new Chaplain[46] is battering away, in the hot sunshine, to a handful of needy souls, but I am too busy, packing medical stores & disposing of sick men, to attend Divine service & should be excused.

I hear that Grant has driven the enemy behind his entrenchments at Richmond, but know not how reliable the word is.[47]

The enemy has attacked & driven in our pickets almost every night since we came here. The outer pickets are ordered to fire on any one approaching them after night, without ever halting them.

They have made several raids on the B. & O. RR. lately, at Martinsburg, Piedmont & Grafton, also captured some of our wagons & horses along the road to this place. They are very bold & fearless; a few hundred of them often attacking a thousand of our men.[48]

The weather seems as sultry & hot as in July, except the evenings which are very cool.

I have nothing more to write,

Good Bye

Alex.

16

Camp near Strasburg, Va.
May 10, 1864

Dear Friends,

Having an opportunity to send a letter back in the morning, I hasten to write you a line.

We arrived here last evening from Winchester, having a very hot day's march, many of our men falling by the way from exhaustion. We are encamped on the hills and in the valleys for a great distance, in the most beautiful country I ever saw. Everything is perfectly lovely and enchanting here this time in the season.

The enemy is reported at Woodstock, some fifteen miles distant up the valley, in great numbers. We were expecting an attack last night, but did not receive it. I suppose, because the rebels did not consider it would be a very healthy operation for them. A bushwhacker shot one of our men, who was grazing a horse near camp last evening. The guilty murderer was caught and will be shot this afternoon by order of Maj. Genl. Sigel. I must hurry and go to witness the execution.

Our signal lights advise us of a great victory on the Rapidan by Grant. Hope and pray it may be true.[49]

Every soldier is in a great glee over the news and brass bands are playing sweet music from every hill.

My Brigade is composed of 12 Va., 1st Va., 34 Mass. and 54 Pa., four as gallant Regiments as ever shouldered a musket.

I am writing this on my knee and our Chaplain a few feet off penning a line, on a little stump, to his "better half."

We have recd. no mail from Martinsburg for about one week, but think we will get our letters before a great while.

Good Bye

Alex.

17

Camp at Strasburg, Virginia
Thursday Evening May 19, 1864

My dear Friends,

I again write to you, having recd. your two last letters this evening, it being the first mail matter I have recd. for about three weeks and I was very glad to hear from you indeed. I recd. also this evening one from John, one from Dr. Riddle and one from Jennie and have just finished reading them.

But to the news. We had a most terrible battle on Sunday 15th inst. at New Market some 32 miles distant up the valley.[50] We marched three days and nights, through rain & storms, without a wink of sleep and hardly a morsel to eat during that time, skirmishing some in the meanwhile with the enemy and driving Imboden's forces[51] before us, halting at Mt. Jackson a moment, we heard heavy cannonading in advance a few miles. We soon learned that Longstreet, Breckinridge and Imboden were fighting our force in advance at New Market some 5 miles distant, so we were ordered up by Sigel on double quick, the rain pouring down in torrents the whole time.[52] We arrived about noon after they had been fighting about two hours with the artillery, the infantry as yet, not having been engaged. When we came up all exhausted & drenched with rain to the skin, the cannons were belching forth their music like the crashing of a thousand thunders, forty two pieces of artillery[53] on our side having opened out and more than that by the enemy; the heavens were literally blackened with shells and canister. My Brigade rushed up to the slaughter pen, and there the volleys of musketry opened out on both sides and was soon most terrific, it being the most hotly contested engagement of the war, many say; lasting from 10 o'clock a.m. until dark, when being outnumbered and overpowered by the enemy, we were compelled to fall back, leaving from fifteen hundred to two thousand of our men dead on the field.[54] Our army was literally routed and defeated. This cannot be denied, but it pains me to say it as I felt so confident of success. But the enemy held the field, getting all our dead and most of the wounded. He drove us back to Mt. Jackson and would have pursued his success and cut us literally to pieces, had we not, after crossing the Shenandoah river, destroyed the bridge which checked his progress as the river was much swollen by recent rains.[55]

I was in the thickest of the fight for about one hour & very much exposed. When we arrived at the field I met the Medical Director who ordered me to proceed immediately upon the field and see to the wounded, getting them in the ambulances &c; accordingly I galloped down on the field, where the minnie [sic] balls and canister were flying like hail and fairly strewing the ground with dead and wounded. My horse became so fractious I could hardly manage him, the noise so terrible and the scene so frightful, the rebels advancing on us like a stone wall, never flinching for a moment, though their ranks were thinned every moment and the ground was covered with their dead and wounded. I never saw braver men than those rebels, they fight worthier of a nobler cause. I saw the color bearer of a South Carolina Regiment, bearing the Palmetto flag, advance fifty paces beyond his Regiment and waving his hat in one hand and holding his colors in the other, he hallored for us to come on. He soon fell with his colors and afterwards, six others in succession with the same colors. Braver men never lived, and though our men occasionally flinched and wavered, they never flinched for one moment. The gallant 34 Mass. & 12 Va. charged on the rebels, and though their General halted them, for he saw the danger of such an attempt, they heeded him not & were rushing into the jaws of death, when Col Wells[56] of the 34th ran forward and caught their color bearer and held him fast and thus checked

Charge of the Corps of Cadets by Benjamin West
Virginia Military Institute

their onward movement. <u>That fatal charge</u> did no good but cost
them the lives of a hundred brave men.[57]

I established, temporarily, a hospital at a little church near
by, and in conjunction with some other Surgeons, did what we

could for the wounded, who were hauled in to us in great numbers. Here I remained about half an hour with about a dozen other surgeons, dressing the wounded & doing the best we could for them, under the circumstances, when another Surgeon came dashing up, saying that we must get away out of the church as speedily as possible, as the lines were changing, the rebels were flanking us and would soon have us surrounded & cut off. I jumped on my horse which I had secured safely in the vestibule of the church, with that of Dr. Holbrook of the 18th Conn., it raining torrents all the time. We ordered the wounded all to be taken further to the rear & dashed down through the fields towards Mt. Jackson, shells flying in all directions over our heads. By this time there was a perfect panic among our troops, which commenced among the cavalry, the rebels having charged upon them. Their officers tried to make them stand, but they would not, but there was an indiscriminate skedaddling of cavalry, infantry & artillery towards Mt. Jackson. Guns & Knapsacks were thrown away; blankets, drums, & musical instruments were pitched away; horses ran riderless over the fields and it seemed that the very gates of pandemonium had opened up and with a sad heart I record that our army met a superior force, in short, fought them for eight long hours, but were finally completely routed and had it had not been for the destruction, by our men, of the bridge over the Shenandoah to cover our retreat, we would have been literally destroyed and I would not have been here tonight. We brought away some two or three hundred of our wounded, filled three hospital buildings in Mt. Jackson and with out whole medical force worked hard with them until some time in the night, many mortally wounded, dying on our hands. We brought away that night over two hundred wounded, all we could furnish transportation for, travelling all night & next day, arriving the next evening on Cedar Creek, some four miles above Strasburg, when we halted to operate on and dress our wounded, and after working all that night & next day until noon, you may imagine how I felt, having to eat but hard tack and a little coffee for five days. I just fell exhausted and slept soundly till next morning. We sent our wounded back to Martinsburg, and then advanced again towards the enemy, going some six miles with a small force where we lay last night, but arose this morning at 1 o'clock, got into line of battle, and then made a retrograde movement back to this place where we are tonight, but have orders to move at $3^1/2$ in the morning, to what place or in what direction I know not. Sigel is very much worried about this disaster but will try and retrieve his good name as early as possible.

I have stated the plain, unvarnished facts in the case as I was present and ought to know some thing about it. I do not know what the newspapers may say about it as we get no papers. They may try to make a victory out of it, but it was as I have told you.

The loss of my own Regiment was pretty heavy, but not as much as that of the 34 Mass., 54th Pa., 1st Va or 123rd Ohio. The last Regiments suffered the most severely, losing a good many of their officers, the most prominent of whom was Lt. Col. Lincoln 34 Mass., a particular friend of mine and a brave man who fell mortally wounded and was left in the Land of the enemy.[58]

The people of this valley are all jubilant over this disaster to our arms and were tickled almost out of their senses at seeing us on our way back. One woman had remarked to me on the road up, that we had a long and bloody road to travel, that disaster after disaster had always befallen our arms in this valley & would always continue so to do, and when we came back she called to me and asked if her prophecy had not been verified, which I could not deny. After the battle that evening I took supper in Mt. Jackson at the same house where last winter I staid all night. They were glad to see me and were so delighted over our reverses of the day, that they would not charge me any thing for my supper, though meals are $5.00 a piece in that town at the present time, thought they only charged me $8.00 last winter for staying all night. I must close lest I weary you. I do not know how I can mail this but will try. Address me via Martinsburg.

18

Strasburg, Va.
May 23, 1864

My dear Friends,

Having an opportunity of sending a letter back by private conveyance I hasten to send you a line.

Genl. Sigel has been superseded by Gen. Hunter[59] who has taken command and issued some awful orders about one thing or another, one is we must fatten our mules and, if necessary, kill them for subsistence. He has cut our transportation down to almost nothing. I have sent my baggage all back to Martinsburg, except one extra shirt which I carry in my saddlebag. I also retain two blankets which I buckle on my horse, behind and I now am ready to gipsey it in earnest.[60]

I wrote you a detailed account of our terrible battle of Sunday week at New Market, which I presume you have received ere this.

Since that day, we have had no general engagement as yet but expect to soon.

I am Yours Truly,

Alex.

19

Camp at Woodstock, Va.
May 27, 1864

Dear Friends,

It being the last opportunity that I shall have, for sometime, perhaps, I embrace it to write you a line letting you know that I am still alive and doing well. We are encamped at the above place, the same camp that we left the 15th inst. to meet the enemy and <u>met</u> him the same day, an account of which I wrote you some days since.

We will make another advance in the morning with our whole force.[61] Sigel is removed and Genl. Hunter now commands the Department.

The weather had been very rainy for some time and we get pretty wet sometimes.

We have recd. glorious news from Grant's army this morning. I sincerely hope that our army may make no more retrograde movements or meet with any more reverses.[62]

My box was duly expressed to you & expressage paid. I hope you have recd. it ere this.

No paymaster yet.

Hoping to hear from you soon I close,

I am yours truly,

Alex.

Your letter of the 18th inst. is the last recd.

Alex.

20

Staunton, Virginia[63]
June 8th 1864

My Dear Friends,

I now have the first opportunity, since my last letter from Woodstock, of relieving your suspense. The federal army now occupies, for the first time, since the rebellion broke out, this

Strong hold of Secession. Time after time, has our army tried to reach this point for the past three years but in vain after sacrificing thousands and thousands of precious lives, until this time, and Genl. Hunter's army has been the one to plant our glorious banner on the ramparts & Staunton, the proud city, the great base of supplies for Richmond, has fallen & the Stars & stripes wave over every public building in the city. But before this was accomplished we passed through another terrible battle, on Sunday June 5th at Piedmont, some eleven miles from here.[64] We moved from Port Republic at daylight that morning meeting the enemy, about 8 o clock in the morning, some 5 miles on this side of the latter place, under command of Maj. Genl. W. E. Jones,[65] when the engagement commenced, and lasted all day until about 4 or 5 o'clock in the evening, completely routing the enemy with great loss on both sides, but the loss was more severe on the rebels, in which they sustained the loss of Genl. Jones who was killed, by a minnie ball [sic] through the head. They also lost a great many other officers and about two or three thousand men killed & wounded. We captured about fifteen hundred prisoners, among whom are sixty-five officers, from Colonels down. We lost in killed & wounded about fifteen hundred to two thousand men.[66]

I was again detailed by the Medical Director to stay on the battlefield & superintend the movements of the Ambulances in taking off the wounded. I was a great part of the time very much exposed, necessarily, to shot & shell which fairly rained around me like hail. A piece of shell knocking off the saddle bags from my saddle, my orderly at the same time having his knapsack shot off his back, as he was riding by my side.

It was the most awful fighting I ever saw, when our boys charged with fixed bayonet, over their barricades, having hand to hand fight. The old 12th Va. leading the charge, lost about a hundred men. I saw many have their brains knocked out with clubbed muskets, but within those ramparts, the rebels threw up their hands by dozens and begged for mercy. Here we took most of our prisoners.[67]

Our boys all acted very gallantly, never flinching, though they were literally mowed down by canister & bullets.

We were busy, all that day & all night & till some time next day gathering the wounded. How heart rending to hear the groans & shrieks of dying men as we went over the battlefield that night with torches, hunting up the wounded. Rebs and Union lay side by side, praying loud & fervently to God to have mercy on them, & when they saw a man with a green sash on,[68] scores of them would beg at the same time for him to help them, but the Surgeon cannot do very much on the field, except to administer a little cordial occasionally or ligate a bleeding artery & see that they are carefully handled by the stretcher bearers.

Our battlefield extended about four miles, which space was strewn with dead & wounded. Of the latter we filled several houses, & barns & established temporary hospitals for our wounded, also the rebs. We brought a great many along with us to Staunton and have sent ambulances after the rest. We will establish a hospital here, at the Deaf & Dumb Asylum, a part of which is now occupied as a Confederate General Hospital, in which are some five hundred rebel wounded from the battle about Richmond. I visited it yesterday morning & got acquainted with about a dozen rebel Surgeons, who are very gentlemanly fellows, but put on a good deal of style. We have paroled all their Surgeons & wounded.

As I write, General Crook & Averell are moving in here from another direction with a large force, & will form a junction with our army to day.[69] Their advance has just arrived. We will all move somewhere soon. I may be detailed at the Hospital, but I hope & pray not. This letter, I think, will go back with the escort & prisoners. I have recd. no mail for two or three weeks. It is all at Martinsburg safe. We subsist on the country, having cut loose from our base, some time ago. Sometime we get nothing to eat for days [remainder of letter missing].

21

Lexington, Va.[70] June 12, 1864

My Dear Friends,

I hasten to scratch you a line. We arrived here last evening & occupy the place, but will move out towards Lynchburg 36 miles distant in the morning. I wrote you from Staunton the account of our battle at Piedmont, on one week from to day.

I recd. on the march yesterday, your two letters, 24 & 26 ult, also 2 papers, the first I had recd. for some time.

We lost in our Regiment, the 12 Va. in the battle of New Market about 50 men and in the battle of Piedmont over 100. You have the pictures of some, Alex Gilmore was killed; Capt. Tomlinson & Lt. Brenneman were wounded. I cannot think of any others, whose pictures you have.

We had a skirmish yesterday before entering the town, but lost only a few men.[71] This is a beautiful town & the seat of the Virginia Military Institute, which we have destroyed by fire to

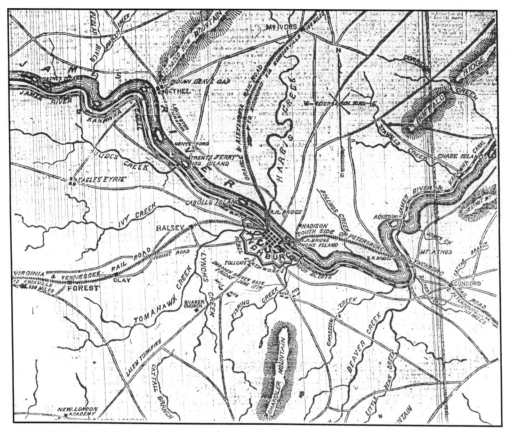

Map of vicinity of Lynchburg, Virginia, for the June 1864 attack on the city by David Hunter.

New York Herald,
June 1864

day, together with all other Government buildings. Hunter's route is marked by ruined walls and piles of ashes. We burn nearly every thing as we go. We also burned the fine residence of Gov. Letcher, to day, also that of Genl. Smith.[72]

We have formed a junction with Crook[73] & Averill[74], in all have about 30,000 men. We had with Sigel about 11,000 men, but only about 4000 were in the fight at New Market.[75] I mention this as you said in your letter that we should not go up the valley with less than 10,000 men. I was at Stonewall Jackson's tomb to day in the Cemetery. It is marked by only a flag staff, on which until yesterday, the Confederate flag waved.[76] We are camped, to night, my Regiment on old Stonewall's farm, near town.

This is the County seat of Rockbridge County and is a very pretty town of considerable wealth. Our army subsists on the country and plunders every thing as it goes along; barns, houses, and stores.[77] Hunter is desperate and will soon stand as high in the rebel estimation as "Beast Butler." I am writing this on rebel paper, ruled both ways to be written on both ways. It sells at 25cts per sheet, Rebel money, but don't [sic] cost us very much. Boarding at the Hotel is $30.00 per day of $10.00 per meal.

The Rebs look down in the mouth & desperate.[78] Woe unto us if we fall into their hands.[79]

They are fortifying at Lynchburg, and we will have a great battle before taking that place.[80]

This is great tobacco country & the boys are loaded down & enough thrown away to pave the streets of Delaware.

Farewell, I send this back by escort for returning wagon train.

Yours Alex

I send you some documents found at Military Institute.

22

Gauley Bridge, Va.
June 29, 1864

My Dear Friends,

I am again, after so long a time, permitted to write you a line, letting you know that I am still alive, as I have no doubt you are by this time, getting very solicitous about my welfare.

I wrote you last from Lexington, some time ago, since which time, our army has passed through the most terrible hardships that flesh is heir to. We marched over the mountains and on to Lynchburg fighting a battle there on the 17th & 18th inst. with a heavy loss to our arms, and were unable to take the place as the enemy recd. heavy reinforcements from Lee's army and he also fought behind fortifications. Genl Hunter thought proper to retire and did so the night of the 18th, bringing several hundred of our wounded with us and establishing a Hospital on the battle field for the remaining.[81] I was detailed by Major Genl. Hunter to take charge of the Hospital, but I did not receive the detail until next day on the march and then it was too late, of which I was very glad, as I could not bear the idea of being left to the mercy of the enemy.[82]

Our march was then by day and by night for seven days, getting no sleep during that time except what I got in the saddle, the enemy fighting us in the rear as far as Salem at which place

Ruins of the Virginia Military Institute

they destroyed and captured, in the mountain gap, twelve pieces of artillery, took two hundred horses, killed several of our men and took several prisoners. We were on the verge of starvation coming over the mountains, the greater part of us getting not a bite to eat for four or five days. Our suffering was almost unendurable, thousands fell by the way to the mercy of the enemy and many starved to death, of these I saw many instances. Out of Genl. Crook's division, eleven hundred fell by the way in crossing the mountains, also over five thousand horses were disbanded and shot and over three hundred wagons had to be destroyed. It was impossible for an army of thirty thousand troops to subsist on the country which we tried to do after leaving Strasburg. Our wagon train was eight miles long and our column of troops six miles in length making fourteen miles of an army which is no small thing. I suffered greatly for something to eat. It was awful, when we saw nothing but starvation before us. I often got off my horse and picked up grains of corn out of the dirt where the cavalry horses had eaten the day before, and I would eat it to keep alive. I saw many an officer offer ten dollars for an ear of corn or half pint of grain to keep starvation away. My health got bad and the mule meat roasted in the fire was perfectly nauseating, but thank God the provision train of hardtack met us yesterday beyond Sewell Mountain and our appetite was appeased and to day about an hour ago we arrived here at Gauley Bridge Kanawaha Co. where we will encamp until tomorrow.[83]

We have seen no papers for 2 or 3 weeks and know nothing of what is going on either in the United States or the Confederacy, but I suppose that this Expedition of Hunter's will be called the greatest, boldest and most desperate of the war.[84] But I must say that I am ashamed to belong to such an army under such a tyrant. Loose rein was given to the soldiers in all kinds of vice, robbery and murder. Every house was plundered of everything, women & children were driven to starvation, their persons violated; many were murdered after homes lain in ashes. I saw many inoffensive citizens murdered in their own yards. I saw many dangling from limbs of trees as I passed along. Villages were destroyed after being plundered, hundreds of private mansions were laid in ashes and great black smokes were arising at all times in the day in all directions. Truly Hunter's path has been one of blood and ashes and to have been taken prisoner from his army would have been death. He is tyrannical to his men. I have seen him horse whip poor wounded soldiers, for some little misdemeanor, with his own hand, until the spark of life had about fled.[85] But he is a brave man and no doubt has accomplished great things on this expedition in the destruction of Railroads & Government property. I can not tell what our loss sums up in the battle before Lynchburg though it counts considerable. My own Regiment lost about 20.

I was on the field all day on the 18th inst. attending to urgent cases & performed a good many operations. I was between the two artillery fires & near my own Regiment which was supporting a Battery. The shells hit among us pretty thick for a while and at one time in the middle of the afternoon the enemy made a charge and a desperate attempt to break our center, which fell back for a time, but soon advanced on them and drove them back. At this time I thought it proper for me to fall back, which I did in a hurry to an old house in the neighborhood, and in a pretty secure position, where I there again established a temporary depot for the reception of wounded to be transferred to the ambulance to the field Hospital.

But there is a mail just going out and I must abruptly close but will write more fully next time.

I know not our destination but we must soon have rest or we will all die.

I have not exaggerated one particle in any of my statements, I think; but have not portrayed it one half.

Yours Truly

Alex

23

On Board Steamer Mason
Kanawaha River, Sunday
July 3, 1864

My Dear Friends,

I again avail myself of the privilege of penning you a line.

I wrote you the other day from Gauley Bridge giving you a brief account of our hardships and privations in "Dixie," a true account of which can never be told. The scenes which I beheld on that expedition, of suffering, no pen can portray and I cannot bear to think of them.

We remained at Gauley Bridge four days and nights resting our men, and left there yesterday morning, arriving at Camp Platt last evening, and embarking this morning, on Steamboats with our Division. Our destination for the present is Parkersburg, then, further I know not.

A great many of our troops are sick, from the hardships of the Campaign, from the effects of which many will never recover.

My own health is only tolerably good, having reduced in flesh very much.

I had a good breakfast on the boat this morning, the first decent meal I have had for two months.

Our fleet of vessels look beautiful, plowing down through the muddy current, as I behold them from my Stateroom.

I read a Cincinnati Commercial of the 30th ult. this morning, the first paper I have seen for a month or more. I see Hon. J. R. Hubbell is nominated for Congress.[86] I am glad of this. I just learn that a mail has arrived. It is being distributed. I must see if I get any thing.

Yes, one letter from home dated June 5th, that's all. I am glad to hear from you. You speak about Uncle Wm. Neil. I have always forgotten to tell you that he has got an heir, by this time 2 or 3 months old. So, Company D, of my Regiment, tells me.

The board shakes so I must stop writing. I will write you soon again.

Truly Alex

U. S. Army

P.S. Another letter for me has turned up in the pile which was overlooked. It is from home dated June 20. The Chaplain just handed it to me.

Chapter II

"Dark Valley of the Shadow of Death"
July 8–December 17, 1864

Hunter's retreat into West Virginia may have saved his army, but unfortunately for Grant's overall strategy, it temporarily placed the Army of West Virginia out of position to cooperate effectively with the Army of the Potomac. Worse still, the retreat left the Shenandoah Valley exposed and uncovered. Therefore, it offered Jubal Early and his pursuing army the opportunity of not only clearing that region of the remaining Union forces there, but in a twist of irony it allowed Lee to turn the tables on Grant by having Early strike into western Maryland and threaten Washington.

Lee had considered the feasibility of applying such pressure in western Virginia as early as April. But mounting pressure on his army by Grant's spring offensive made such a move risky. Yet, Hunter's success in the Valley at Piedmont and his continued advance up the Valley, which seriously threatened Southern supply centers and lines of communication, could not be ignored and forced a decision. Fortunately for Lee, the bloody repulse of the Army of the Potomac at Cold Harbor and Grant's decision to move south of the James River temporarily afforded him a respite. Lee could risk detaching a corps to strike at Hunter in western Virginia. On June 12 he ordered Lieutenant General Jubal Early to hold his Second Corps in readiness to march to the Valley. He hoped that Early could trap and deliver a decisive blow to Hunter's rear and then, if possible, to advance down the Shenandoah Valley and over the Potomac River to threaten Washington.

Portrait of General Jubal Early (C.S.A), circa 1865, after the war.

General Philip Sheridan (center) and his staff.

Early's men, behind a veil of secrecy, were quickly in motion on the following day. His route stretched from the Richmond defenses to Louisa Court House and finally to Charlottesville. There he planned to turn westward and move into the Valley through either Brown's or Swift Run Gaps.[1] Initially Early, ignorant of Hunter's whereabouts, needed intelligence. A Federal cavalry raid on the Orange & Alexandria Railroad had temporarily interrupted the lines of communication between Charlottesville and Lynchburg. Lacking reports on Federal movements in western Virginia, Early assumed that Hunter was still in the Valley. However, on his arrival at Charlottesville he learned that the Army of West Virginia was advancing towards Lynchburg. Galvanized into action, Early soon had Major General Stephen D. Ramseur's Division and part of Brigadier General John B. Gordon's Division on the cars of the Orange & Alexandria Railroad headed for Lynchburg. His decisiveness and shrewd tactics in combating the Union forces saved the city from capture.

Hunter, overestimating the size of the Confederate reinforcements and fearing his increasing shortage of supplies and ammunition, decided to retreat. Despite a vigorous pursuit by Early, Hunter managed to escape into the mountains and back into West Virginia. After breaking off the chase at "Hanging Rock," the question for Early was now whether to return with his corps to the Army of Northern Virginia or to proceed down the Valley in order to carry out Lee's original proposal. He alone had the necessary judgement to decide. In a telegram to Early the Confederate commander left it entirely up to his discretion. Early "determined to take the responsibility of continuing it."[2] After a short rest his small army marched briskly and enthusiastically down the Shenandoah Valley towards Winchester, Martinsburg and the Potomac River.

After capturing Martinsburg, the Confederates fanned out into western Maryland. Easily sweeping through that region, they collected ransoms at Hagerstown and Frederick. An attempt to halt the Southerners at the Monocacy River, a few miles east of Frederick, by General Lew Wallace with a small army failed badly. The route to Washington lay open.[3] On reaching the outskirts of the capital, Early merely probed and threatened the city's defenses for two days and then quietly slipped back into Virginia. Returning to the Valley, Early, always a master chessman, continued to pose a threat to western Maryland and southern Pennsylvania for the remainder of the summer.

Hunter and his army, temporarily out of position in West Virginia, played no role in countering the Confederate raid on Washington. Even after Early's return to the Valley in July, the Army of West Virginia offered an ineffective foil to Southern operations in that region. Hunter's incompetence was painfully underscored by the Confederate raid on Chambersburg, Pennsylvania, in late July. The burning of the town by Southerners in retaliation for Hunter's actions in Virginia seriously embarrassed the Federal government. The Southern challenge to Federal control in the region demanded a change in leadership. The War Department appointed General Philip H. Sheridan to the command of four combined departments.[4] Grant's instructions to Hunter's successor charged him simply "to put himself south of the enemy and follow him to the death." Not only did Grant want the destruction of Early's army, but a prime objective, as he informed Sheridan, "In pushing up the Shenandoah Valley . . . it is desirable that nothing should be left to invite the enemy to return."[5]

Yet Sheridan, aware of the possible adverse political ramifications of a military reverse in the Valley on the November presidential election, cautiously waited for the proper moment to strike Early a decisive blow. On September 19, after receiving information that

Kershaw's division and Cutshaw's artillery had been recalled to Richmond, Sheridan attacked Early at Winchester.[6] Seriously defeated, the Confederates retreated to Fisher's Hill, outside of Strasburg. Sheridan's victory, beginning with Winchester and ending at Cedar Creek, initiated a month of fierce fighting for control over the Valley. In a desperate Southern gamble on October 19, Early struck back at the Union commander. The element of surprise initially pointed to a stunning victory, but sadly for Early, such hopes quickly faded in devastating defeat. The Federal victory at Cedar Creek ended the contest for dominance over the Shenandoah. After that, Early's shattered army could offer only token resistance. By the end of the year, with the Valley secure, Grant had the luxury of shifting a sizeable portion of Sheridan's army to aid the siege of Petersburg and the final push on Lee and Richmond.

1

Green Springs, Va., B & O. Rail Road
12 miles east of Cumberland, Md.
July 8, 1864

My Dear Friends,

We are again back on the old B. & O. Road after rebels. They have again invaded Maryland and torn up the railroad and played smash generally, took possession of Martinsburg, & Harper's Ferry, captured all our baggage at the former place and Sigel & Mulligan have given them a fight.[7] We can get no reliable particulars at present. We have already rebuilt one bridge over North Branch near Cumberland and have crossed over with our trains and are now at another bridge awaiting its finish which will be in a few hours. I am writing this on board the cars. We have Sullivan's Division with us. As fast as the rebels tore up road, we can lay down.

I wrote you last from on board a Steamer on the river. We landed our troops on the afternoon of July 4th at the foot of Blennerhassett Island on the Ohio Shore, as the boats could run no further on account of low water.[8] We were then obliged to walk about six miles to Parkersburg, as we had sent our horses across the country from camp Piatt to Parkersburg. You can't believe how glad I was to once more put my foot on Ohio shore. As we footed it up through Ohio along the shore we were greeted from every house by flying banners and white handkerchiefs. We halted to eat cherries and berries and pies & cakes & to drink milk which were freely given to us all along the road; halted at a picnic, for it was the glorious 4th, and though we looked hardened and bronzed from the effects of that terrible campaign, yet they gathered around us and welcomed us. How thankful I felt that I was again in Ohio, as I never expected, at one time, to see her again. We staid in Parkersburg one night and left the morning of the 5th on board the cars, arriving here last evening.

The men of the Command are very badly used up and many, very many, will never recover from the great Hunter raid. Hunter's dispatch is a pack of lies from beginning to end. He had no loss, he says, of Government property, when in fact, five millions of dollars will not cover our loss. He also says that his loss of men was about six hundred, when five thousand is too low an estimate. My own division started with 7,900 men and at present can only sum up 3,500. The divisions of Averell, Crook, Duffie, & Stahel, all lost heavily.[9]

I know something about this as it is part of my business to make out lists of killed & wounded.

I have heard at least a hundred officers declare that they will resign, unless Hunter is removed. Indeed he is very unpopular among officers & men.[10]

I never mentioned that during our raid, we visited all the pleasant resorts of Virginia, such as Blue, Salt, and White Sulphur, Hot, Warm & Sweet Springs, Natural bridge, Peaks of Otter, Weirs Cave and many other caves. Crossed all the ranges of the Alleghenies four times, the ranges of the Blue Ridge twice and travelled all over the great Valley of Virginia from beginning to end.

I have never had any time to write any thing like a descriptive letter or I could have told a good many things that would interest you.

It seems that there is not much rest in store for us, but I think we will not leave this rail road very far soon. I am very needy for money. I wish you would send me 10$, soon. My clothes are all in rags and am almost hatless & bootless; though they say I am the best dressed man in the Command. My health is getting better, and will soon be stout again. You had perhaps better address me Martinsburg and I will get it. I think a Paymaster will be apt to visit us soon & pay us six months pay, hope so at least.

Hoping to hear from you soon,

I close Truly Alex.

2

Martinsburg, Va. July 12, 1864

My dear Friends,

I am again at my old stomping grounds after a long round of over a thousand miles and after having endured many privations and hardships. We arrived here yesterday with the advance of Hunter's army, driving the rebels out before us and killing some. The rebel army has again invaded Maryland with upwards of thirty thousand strong and are committing all kinds of depredations & crimes in retaliation for Hunter's raid.[11]

Those that passed through Martinsburg plundered every body, friend and foe, and made great boasts. The railroad has been cut up pretty badly, but we have it about all repaired again.

I do not know what our army will do, what our destination, or how soon we will move, but I think the rebs will make a sorry raid of it to themselves if they do not escape soon, as they have to contend with the armies of Lew Wallace, Couch, Sigel, & Hunter, who will press them closely.

The citizens here were overjoyed yesterday on our arrival, and flags & banners waved from every loyal house, and many happy greetings and cordial shake of hands were bestowed upon us. I was nearly pulled in two at my old boarding; they were so glad to see me. How sad to think that many, <u>very many</u> of our brave men who left here in April did not return, but are bleaching their bones on Southern soil.

Most of the Government stores were shipped from this place and saved. Yet a great deal fell into the rebel's hands, amongst the latter the officers' baggage, which was plundered.[12] However my baggage was saved by some friend carrying it to my old boarding house & hiding it. I was surprised to find it.

I suppose you are reading a great deal these times about Hunter's "great raid". Hunter has shut down a good many newspapers on account of their telling the truth, but the latter "is mighty & will prevail."[13]

I should like to hear from you soon. I wrote you the other day from Green Springs, in which I state that I should be pleased to be the recipient of 10$, as finances are very low.

I think as soon as we get settled the Paymaster will soon be round and liquidate our claims.

Address me

Martinsburg, Va.

Truly

Alex

3

Near Leesburg Va. July 17, 1864

Dear Friends,

We moved from Martinsburg the 13th Inst. on to Harper's Ferry, thence to Berlin near Point of Rocks, here fording the Potomac we made rapidly on to this point. We have had some fighting for two days with the retreating rebel army. Yesterday we destroyed & captured quite an amount of the rebel wagon train and took a number of prisoners. They are making away with as much celerity as possible and we are after them with Hunter's army.

Genl. Crook commands our division now, Genl. Sullivan having been relieved and in charge of post at Harper's Ferry.

I understand that our division is to report to and become a part of the 6th Army Corps under Genl. Wright.[14]

For the past two weeks I have been detached from my command and in charge of 2nd Md. Potomac Brigade. I hope to be relieved soon.

The weather is pleasant, though very dusty. My health is very good which I hope may continue so.

The old "Johnny rebs" are getting the worst of their great raid.

I hope they may all sink into Hell before they get back.

I do not know our destination, have no idea.

I have not heard from home for a long time, but hope you are flourishing & well.

I enclose one of Genl. Breckinridge's general orders, which I captured yesterday. I hope to hear from you soon. Address me as usual.

Truly Thine

Alex.

4

Snicker's Ferry, Shenandoah River, Va.
July 21, 1864

My Dear Friends,

I wrote you last from near Leesburg; soon after that we moved
on towards this point, followed closely in the rear by the Sixth
Army Corps, the ball opening out on the 18th Inst. at this Ferry,
between Generals Crook & Early, the latter having some five divisions constituting about thirty thousand men. Our troops
fought with desperation, but were at first repulsed and driven
into the river, many of whom drowning. I made a very narrow
escape from being cut off by the enemy's sharp shooters, whose
guns commanded the river, when we fell back, the river being so
deep that my horse was obliged to swim. I saw more than a
hundred men drown in the river. We lost in the engagement
some five or six hundred in killed & wounded, the enemy losing
heavier, the fight closing at dark on the 18th inst. The next day,
he lay on one side of the river, we on the other, having been
reinforced the night previous by the Sixth & parts of the nineteenth and third Corps, amounting to twenty five thousand men.
This reinforcement in addition to our force of about twenty thousand men, made a very handsome army. On the 19th inst. we
were very busing caring for the wounded, that we were fortunate enough to get back across the river, amounting to some
three hundred, the rest falling into the enemy's hands, many of
these we got to day, the rebels having carried them off to different localities.[15]

I have just returned with a train of ambulances loaded, having been sent by the Medical Director, this morning with a flag
of truce, in search of our wounded; many of these I found in the
woods in squads of 15 or 20, in different places. The rebel soldiers first having robbed them of every thing, even their hats,
boots, & coats. We have shipped them all to Harper's Ferry this
evening.

Many of our dead, the rebels left naked on the field, every
stitch of clothing having been taken, some whom they pretended
to bury, were only half buried, heads & feet both sticking out of
the ground. Instances of this kind I have seen often before, a
disgrace to any civilized race. They bury their own dead very
neatly, putting up very nice head boards.

The night of the 19th, they threw some shells from their side of the river, over into our camp, disturbing our slumber somewhat, but our batteries replied to them right musically, and the next morning the 20th, on feeling, we found the enemy had flown & Genl. Duffie after him, also the sixth & nineteenth corps, the latter returning last night, just after we had crossed.

On the 19th about the middle of the afternoon when I was very busy in the field Hospital with other Surgeons, a Surgeon of the 6th Army Corps, slipped up and laying his hand on my shoulder, said, "How are you Alexander"?; I turned around and grasped the hand of my Cousin Dr. Riddle of the 61st Pa. of which he is Asst. Surgeon. Indeed we were both much pleased to see each other, after a separation of some eight years. The Doctor looks well and hearty and is extremely jolly. Our Brigade Head Quarters in the field for a day or two were not over 200 yards apart, and we had quite a pleasant visit. The sixth Corps left us last evening for some other point and we are again separated.

Tell John & Sattie that the day I left Martinsburg the (13th) I took dinner with Sattie's own cousin & also visited her own Aunt (her father's sister). I happened that day tò think father Hedges told me last winter, that he had a sister living in Martinsburg, by the name of Reid, so I called on Mrs. James H. Reid her son whom I had been acquainted with for sometime, never dreaming during that time that he was Sattie's own Cousin. He is a man 40 years old & has a nice family. His mother, old Mrs. Reid, resides with her daughter & son-in-law, Mr. & Mrs. Sayles, about one mile from town on the Charlestown road. I called on them and informed them that my brother had married the old lady's niece & the daughter's cousin and that my brother was virtually that latter's cousin and the former's nephew. Old Mrs. Reid is about 70 yr. old and quite childish, though she was pleased to hear from her brother Elijah's family.

I showed them Sattie's photograph and left them one of mine. Mr. Sayles lives in fine style & I think is wealthy. They have a very beautiful daughter of some 17 summers. At Hedgesville 8 miles from Martinsburg, I have often seen the old stone mansion in which old man Hedges was born.

My short stop was very pleasant, but the troops were moving and I was obliged to tear myself away. I hope to be able to renew my acquaintance in the future.

The last letter from home was dated about the middle of June & recd. on board the Steamboat. I expect there are a good many coming on the way, but we have recd. no mail since that on the boat, but hope to soon.

I do not know what our destination is, and the last newspaper was Baltimore American of the 8th inst. I know not what is going on in the outer world. Hope to see daylight soon. I must lay down on the ground & sleep as it is getting late, & I was up all last night with the wounded. Write soon as before to.

Alex.

Later

Winchester, Va. July 23, 1864

We moved on to this city from Snicker's Ferry, arriving her last night, & now I will try to finish my letter which I have had no opportunity of sending back yet. Yesterday morning I recd. from home two letters, one of the 6th inst. to Parkersburg, the other of 14th containing 10$, which I was glad to receive.

It seems you have failed to receive some of my letters, one from Lexington Va. containing an account of the destruction of the Military Institute, Genl. Smith's & Gov. Letcher's houses, and many other items of interests, also my letter from Gauley detailing our two days battle before Lynchburg, the disastrous retreat of our forces, the starvation & suffering of our troops, the forced march of one week day and night without bathing, &c. &c. 'Tis strange my letter should have become lost. I also sent you some interesting documents from the archives of the Military Institute, which I suppose were lost. I preserved one large Unabridged Dictionary (Websters) which I have along in the wagon, but will ship first opportunity. I made one good black horse, saddle & bridle, by the raid, and had I only transportation, might have made thousands of dollars.

You ask about Joel Hull. His Regt., the 91st Ohio, was with us on the raid to Lynchburg. 'Tis strange I never saw him. I got acquainted with their Surgeons and some other officers. I can't tell whether he is along now with us or not. I will enquire.

You speak about resignation; this I have no notion of at present, but expect to stick it out to the last. I have already, and I find this day is the anniversary of the date of my commission, had more experience than some of the oldest practitioners in civil practice and particularly in the branch of operative Surgery have had a fine field of experience.

I forgot to mention that in our last battle we had our Surgeon killed, and Providence favored us that more were not killed.

The casualties fell particularly heavy on our officers, losing a good many, among them some half dozen colonels. The rebels lost one General and several colonels.

Battle of Winchester

Engraving by A. R. Waud

The rebs are in mass at Strasburg and I expect we move immediately upon them. We are falling in. I must stop, good by. Write to Martinsburg.

Alex.

5

Maryland Heights, Md.
July 28, 64

My Dear Friends,

I am again permitted to address you, after another sanguinary struggle.

I wrote you from Winchester about our battle at Snicker's Ferry on the 18 inst. and about our army moving on to Winchester, in pursuit of the rebel army.

On Saturday & Sunday, July 23 & 24th, we fought another terrible battle which ended on the afternoon of the 24th with great disaster to our arms & was complete rout of our army. When the fighting of the first day ended, both armies in statu quo, we had flattered ourselves that he fled in the night, but in addition to his thirty thousand men of the first day, he received that night a reinforcement of twenty five thousand men, the latter perhaps as many men as we had altogether in the fight & they worn out and in no fighting condition.[16]

Our troops fought bravely until about 4 P.M. Sunday when the enemy massing a heavy force on our left suddenly flanked us, coming up almost in the rear, pouring into our ranks a galling fire of musketry, grape and canister, our men breaking & running in confusion, the ground literally strewn with our dead & wounded. 'Twas here the brave Mulligan (of Lexington notoriety) commanding the division of the left, fell pierced by three bullets. He stood where no other man would stand, with hat in hand, trying to rally his men. Five men were shot down, in trying to recover his body & it was abandoned. A little to the right of this, the ranks of the 12th Va. were being thinned every moment by a leaden hail too hot & heavy for any but patriot martyrs to withstand, here our brave and gallant Col. Curtis & Maj. Brown fell prisoners to the rebel host who swept forward like an avalanche.

At this time I with a number of other surgeons had established a little depot for wounded immediately in the rear of our brigade, in a narrow strip of woods, the shells from both sides passing over our heads. To this point, mangled heroes were borne by scores on stretchers, where giving them temporary aid & dressing, we shipped them off to the field hospital in ambulances. I was dressing the shattered arm of Col. Young of 20 Pa. Cavly. when the panic among our troops commenced, rushing down like an avalanche on us. I was obliged to change my position several times in a few minutes to save my life, finally throwing the Col. on a horse & we made good our escapes just in time. At this time the fields were literally covered by our troops fleeing in confusion, with the rebel hosts right at their heels.

We got off several hundred of our wounded, but all our dead & nearly all our wounded fell into his hands.

The panic commenced about 3 miles from Winchester, and whilst our cavalry checked them for a moment in the suburbs of the city, myself and another doctor dismounted and ran into my old friend Mother Grimms to get a bite to eat. We had only eaten about ½ doz. bites when the boy who watched our horses, ran in and told us that in order to save our bacons we must dash out immediately as the rebel cavalry were [sic] just making a charge into town. We did so just as they charged, but having two hundred yards the start of them we left them behind, though the balls buzzed over our heads plentifully all the way down the street. Several shells from rebel artillery struck in the street near us, some of them going into the houses.

From that on I rode with the ambulances. We hauled at Bunker Hill that night, the enemy also stopping in our rear. The next day, we arrived at Martinsburg all in confusion, our troops scattered to the four winds & no organized command. They fought us in the streets of Martinsburg, many women & children being killed here by their artillery. We moved on crossing the Potomac that evening at Williamsport Md. Here the enemy seems to have taken another route. I know not.

We moved on by way of Sharpsburg with our demoralized Command arriving at these Heights yesterday forenoon.

It was a great victory to the rebels, they capturing several thousand prisoners & a great deal of our artillery.[17] We are now resting our weary bodies on these heights under the guardian protection of these terrible guns.

I know not where the rebels are now or what we shall do. No words can portray the scenes that occurred on Sunday at Winchester nor, had I the power or time, would I want to make them public. Such a terrible disaster to our arms; Bull Run is no where, those say, who were in both. I cannot write you any particulars as I am so hurried.

I saw Lt. Joel Hull 91st Ohio, yesterday. He is well, tell Mrs. Hull.

The trains are all suspended from the west. This must go by Baltimore. The road is again torn up west.

Truly,

Alex.

6

Frederick City, Maryland
Aug. 4, 1864

My Dear Friends,

I again write you, having written you last from Maryland Heights, after which we moved up the Shenandoah Valley to Halltown near Charlestown where we lay two nights during which time we were reinforced again by the 6th and 19th army Corps who had been on a visit to Washington City, but the exigencies of the times causing them to return to us again.[18] There I fell in which my old friend & cousin Dr. Riddle again who was enjoying himself finely. He sends his kind regards to you all. He had just heard from home where they were all well. Uncle Alex. is keeping a grocery and doing pretty well. We moved back from Halltown Saturday, via Harper's Ferry through Pleasant Valley Md. to within a short distance of the Pennsylvania line at Wolfsville where we lay two days, & moving from there yesterday we arrived at this City last evening, the 6th & 19th Corps going in the advance. This is a very pretty City of ten thousand inhabitants, most of whom are very loyal.[19]

During the rebel raid, a levy of two hundred thousand dollars (200,000) was made on the city and promptly responded to, as failing to do this, the city was to be laid in ashes.[20]

A great sensation has been produced among the rebel sympathizers by a recent order from Genl. Hunter, sending all of this class south of the lines and confiscating their property.[21]

I find here an old Class-mate of mine, Harry Marky who belongs to one of the F'.F'.'s. Poor Harry, after spending 5 years within the dingy walls of college among the classics and ancient lore and receiving the degree of A.B. has embarked in the lumber business with his father, and earning an honest livelihood.

Well, we are here with a pretty big army and our destination I know not. I think that the second rebel raid is about played out. I suppose you had read all about the burning of

Chambersburg Pa. &c., &c.[22] Our mail has not come to hand yet & I have recd. no letters lately.

Truly,

Alex.

7

At Foot of Md. Heights
near Sandy Hook, Md.
Sunday Aug. 7, 1864

Dear Friends,

I again write you having written you last from Frederick City where we lay 2 or 3 days, then moving on to this place yesterday. From all appearances, it seems that we are preparing for another grand raid or some terrible movement. Grant has been with us for a day or two, closeted with our Generals, planning some great scheme or giving us the benefit of his wise counsels.[23] We have already a large army here and more are joining us. We have besides Hunter's old army, the 19th, 13th & 6th army corps, and as I write, Sheridan's Cavalry are moving up the first plateau in clouds of dust. I believe the design is to thoroughly clear this country of the invading army, & destroy them effectively in their route up the Shenandoah Valley.

This valley, 150 miles in length and 30 miles in breadth, containing natural resources unequalled, constitutes the great granary of the Southern Confederacy and I think it policy for our government to do what they never have done; throw into this valley an army sufficiently large to hold it against all attempts on the part of the enemy. We should even occupy Staunton, as Buffalo Gap, near that city, is the great key to the valley.

I am worn down with chronic diarrhoea, but will go as long as possible.

I have not enjoyed an exception from this complain since I was at Lynchburg. Very many of the troops of our command are affected the same way.

I think it probable that we march tomorrow from this point. Living is very high at fabulous prices. We buy from the cheapest place, our commissary & pay for Ham per pound 28 cts, Sugar 24, Coffee 55, Hard tack 8., and every thing in proportion, a great part of the time we having nothing but Coffee & Hard tack. No Paymaster yet, and finances in bad condition. We have all borrowed until played out & no money in the command. Please send me another little drip of money.

Address as before, Alex.

8

Camp Army of West Virginia at Cedar Creek
Near Strasburg, Va., Shenandoah Valley
Aug. 15, 1864

My Dear Friends,

I again write you though I have not heard from home for a long time. I do not know why I can receive no mail. However I did receive a letter from John some few days ago. Perhaps I may receive my letters soon, all in a pile.

I wrote you last from Pleasant Valley I think, soon after which we moved up the valley, the whole Command under Maj. Genl. Sheridan who recently assumed command of four Departments,[24] our corps under Maj. Genl Crook moved in a very covered and circuitous route along the Shenandoah river, making a flank movement, whilst the main army moved in several columns up different roads. We engaged the enemy first near Newtown,[25] skirmishing very lively from that point to this Creek.

Our force now amounts to about seventy five thousand (75,000) men, and we now lay side by side by the great rebel army of Early who was reinforced night before last by Longstreet with about 40,000 additional troops. During the last 3 days we have had more or less fighting, though no general engagement as yet.[26]

Our two great armies lay about ¾ of a miles apart & at present are fortifying. The country is so open & hilly we can see the rebels distinctly throwing up dirt on Fisher's Hill and sitting around leisurely smoking their pipes and eating their grub. My Regiment & the 1st Va. made a gallant charge night before last on the rebels, drawing their skirmishers in and killing a good many. The 12th lost 10 men yesterday in guarding our Signal Corps on the mountain. The rebel Signal is flying on Round Top Mountain[27], & all the skirmishing and fighting is distinctly seen. 'Tis a beautiful thing to see a fight ¹/₂ a mile off. I saw last evening a splendid cavalry charge, from where I am writing, and as I now write, the musketry is banging away & an occasional ball passes over our heads.

The gallant old 12th Va. is "growing smaller by degrees & beautifully less", starting out in the Spring Campaign with 950 men, we now only number about 300 effective men. Our many sanguinary struggles this summer have told on us & hundreds of our brave Regiment are bleaching their bones on Southern soil or pining away in Southern prisons. I am thankful that amongst these many scenes of carnage & the many privations & hardships of this campaign, I yet live & enjoy pretty good health.

Dr. Riddle called at my Hd. Quarters yesterday & made me quite a visit. Whilst he was here, our Chaplain preached a very impressive discourse. He took advantage of the occasion to make an impression, as quite a lively fight was progressing about $1/2$ a mile off at the same time, which we could distinctly see, & as men were dropping in line of battle with the enemy, he told them to behold their comrades falling in the agonies of death & to consider the uncertainty of life, that in this midst of life we are in death."

But my opinion is that such sermons are calculated to intimidate the soldiers, notwithstanding the moral lessons they may contain. As I write my Regiment is just moving out on the skirmish line & before night many of them may fall. But these things I have got used to . I can now lie down & take a knap [sic] during a battle, & take it cool. Balls whistle over my head every day and I hardly notice them.

Good bye

Address me

Harper's Ferry, Va.

& it will follow me.

Truly Alex.

9

Sheridan's Army 3 miles from Bolivar Heights
August 23rd 1864

My Dear Friends,

I wrote you last from Cedar Creek about a week since, soon after which our army fell back through Winchester, tarrying for short periods at Clifton & Charlestown, yesterday morning arriving at this place, Sunday, near Charlestown the 6th and 19th Corps fought the enemy, though had no general engagement. We fell back from that point to this, drawing the rebel army after us, and are now nicely fortified, our grand army's right resting on the Potomac, the left on the Shenandoah.[28] Whenever we stop now a days, the first work is to throw up breast works and it is wonderful the amount of work a large army can do in a short space of time in the way of throwing up works and building abbattis [sic], and as I write, the sound of the axe, pick, and shovel click in all directions, strengthening our center.

For the last ten days we have had fighting every day, more or less until we have got used to it. Yesterday there was fighting all along our lines, but no general engagement. About 4 o'clock in the evening two of our brigades via the left made a very sneakful charge on the enemy's right driving them, killing & surrounding many and capturing quite a number. This morning against day light brisk skirmishing commenced and has been kept up all day thus far (9 o'clock A.M.) all along the lines and as I write, our battery has opened out from our center & makes the woods ring with her 12 pounders. I am now seated under a tree not 50 yards from this battery and I can fully appreciate all her noise. As soon as the Johnnies reply to this I shall be compelled to light out to a more secure retreat. "How use doth breed a man", for what would once have disturbed my nervous equilibrium has no effect now on me and I now lie down every night in line of battle, and sleep as sweetly on the hard ground to be awaked by the booming of cannon or sound of musketry, as though I slept at home in a feather bed.

My health has got first rate again and am now as well as ever. Your letter of Aug. 12, enclosing $10, I recd., also one from mother of the 2nd inst. Your letter to Frederick, I have not recd. yet.

I am very much pleased to hear of your nomination for the office.[29] You should have had long ago, and I sincerely hope there may be no impediment to your election.

I have recd. two letter from John lately, one of which I have answered.

I have recd. no pay yet, our army has been in such a state of transition, but could get my pay if I only could get to the Ferry, as Paymasters are there. Watch the newspapers for Sheridan's army & you will see what we are doing.

Address me soon to Harper's Ferry Va.

Alex.

10

Head Quarters Middle Department
In the Field near Bolivar, Va.
August 27, 1864

My Dear Friends,

Having a moment's leisure this morning I shall drop you a line informing you that my health is very good, and am enjoying myself very well.

We are having more or less fighting here every day along different parts of our line. Casualties on our side amounting to from one hundred to six hundred every day. Yesterday morning, the skirmishers on both sides, immediately in front of our division, agreed on an armistice for several hours. "Johnny Reb" hallows over & says to our boys, "No use of this firing all the time, supposing we stop, I want to get my breakfast. We will agree to stop if you will and let us get our breakfasts." Yank hallors back, "All right have you got any tobacco to trade for coffee? Let's throw down our guns and meet half way." And nearly all day the boys were meeting half way & making exchanges of various little articles. What a pity such good friends, should meet in deadly conflict every day.

We have a heavy force, behind entrenchments reaching from the Shenandoah to the Potomac, our left on the former, our right on the latter, a distance of 7 or 8 miles.

I understand this morning that Early is falling back. If this be the case I expect we shall follow after.[30] You must examine the papers for particulars as I have not time to specify particulars.

I see a great many things to write about every day, but really I have not the time nor is this any place to concentrate one's thoughts on any thing.

I feel very confident that we have force sufficient to prevent any more raids or indeed to meet any thing short of Lee's whole army. I think Sheridans army cannot fall short in numbers of Seventy five thousand and of these we have twenty thousand cavalry.

I must close

Write soon to Harper's Ferry

Truly,

Alex.

11

Charlestown, Va.
Sept 1, 1864

Dr. Friends,

I am quite well; have recd. recently all your back letters and papers for which I thank.

The Paymasters are here and this morning I was paid, & after paying all my debts & retaining a good amount, I will express you this day, 725$ which I hope you will receive.

Our army is still lying here. The recent movements of Grant on the Weldon Rail Road having necessitated the recalling by Lee, of Early, to the defenses of Richmond. The general supposition is that he is leaving the Valley.[31]

We moved last Sunday morning from our entrenchments at Bolivar to this point; have had since more or less fighting every day, to the great danger of Early's army.

I am in great hurry to go to Harper's Ferry, ten miles distant, to express my money.

Dr. Riddle sends his kind regards. Uncle Alex. is keeping a grocery & doing pretty well.

Hoping you are well.

I close

Truly

Alex.

12

Sheridan's Army
Berryville, Va.
Tuesday Eve. Sept. 6, 1864

My Dear Friends,

Your letter of the 29th ult. is just received and was gladly welcomed by me. I wrote you last Sept. 1st from Charlestown Va.; also the same day remitted to you by Express $725.00 which I trust you have recd. ere this and appropriated as you may deem proper.

On Saturday Sept 3rd our army moved by day light from Charlestown, and had an engagement the same afternoon near where we are now encamped. The battle was very hot and lasted till long after dark. They made a very stubborn resistance and fought very bravely, but our forces held the field, punishing him very severely, killing & wounding many and taking a good many prisoners, mostly Mississippi troops who, in making a desperate charge on Crook's Center, came a little too far, & were completely surrounded & captured.[32]

A Rebel Captain asked me if I had heard from the Chicago Convention & the result. I told him I had & that McClellan was nominated by the "Peace Party." He thought they had a strange fancy for a peace man to nominate such a man as McClellan. He did not call him a peace man by any means.[33]

I had a Baltimore American in my packet of that day's issue, which contains the news of Atlanta's surrender. This I handed to the Captain whose countenance somewhat fell on reading the news. He said that "their people might as well give up now as any time, no use of being so stubborn about it." He is a graduate of Yale College & a very smart fellow. He found a classmate here in the 18th Conn. vols.

We have thrown up formidable breast works here; also the rebels are entrenched a short distance from here on the Opequon river.[34]

I do not know whether we will follow them any further or not. The weather is very rainy & disagreeable and the nights miserable to put in on the cold wet ground. I did not sleep any last night. It rained on me all night & wet me through.

I sympathize with you in your trouble with James. Hope he may get better.

'Tis dark & raining. I must close.

Write soon as usual,

Truly,

Alex.

13

Sheridan's Army
Summit Point, Va.
Sept. 9th 1864

My Dear Friends,

I again write you, informing you of my whereabouts, also that I am very well. I wrote you last from Berryville. We moved from that point which was our extreme left, to this place, our extreme right, on yesterday.

Here is where we fought the battle of Charlestown on the 21st ult.[35]

Early is still confronting us with a large army. He certainly cannot subsist his army much longer and will have to withdraw his army, before a great while.

We are much encouraged by our recent successes in the South and our soldiers are still more strongly in favor of the re-election of "Honest Abe."

I do not think that McClellan will get the support of a corporal's guard in Sheridan's army.

We cannot see the propriety of compromising with a thing that is on its last legs, a pretty time to elect a "Peace Candidate"!, the only peace I want, is an "honorable peace" with no concessions on our part.

I merely write to let you know that I am very well & enjoying myself finely.

Our Major came up to day having escaped from the rebels after the battle of Winchester by fleeing to the mountains.

I also forgot to mention some time ago that Col. Curtis escaped from them, rejoining his command at Pleasant Valley.[36]

I have not heard from you for some few days, but expect to as soon as the mail comes up from the Ferry.

I enclose a few morphine powders to give James when he becomes restless.

Hoping to hear from you soon & often I am

Yours Truly

Alex.

14

Summit Point, Va.
Sept. 14, 1864

My Dear Friends,

I am just in receipt of Uncle Wm. Neil's letter of the 5th inst. which I was very glad to receive. This I will answer to his home at Valley Grove.

He says my last letter to you recd. was of the 27th ult. I have written several letters to you since that which I presume you have recd. before this.

I have received no letters very lately from you but hope to soon, though our mail is very irregular, having to come by way to Baltimore, and lay some days at Harper's Ferry before it comes up to the army by way of the supply wagon trains, a distance of some 18 miles.

A large mail for this command was captured a day or two since, enroute from Harper's Ferry to this place. I may possibly have lost some letters by the capture.

We had quite a battle yesterday, though our corps was not engaged.[37] The enemy, the principle part, is entrenched in our front on the Opequon, Early having his Head Quarters in Winchester. How long they will remain here I am unable to say, but think that they cannot subsist their army much longer so far away from their base of supplies. The rainy season has opened out in earnest, it having poured down good & strong for several days, making it very disagreeable soldiering, and particularly sleeping at night on the wet ground, with scarcely any shelter and a solitary blanket for a cover. Hope this may be over soon and we get some kind of quarters.

I have no particular news to write and therefore will close my letter.

Hoping to hear from you soon, I close,

Truly Yours,

Alex.

15

Sheridan's Army
Camp near Summit Point, Va.
Sept. 16th 1864

My Dear Friends,

All still quiet on the Opequon and upper Potomac, and we are still confronted by Early and the fifty thousand gentlemen under his command.[38] Why we do not assume the offensive and drive these vandals from this beautiful valley I am unable to say, unless Sheridan's policy be to keep Early here as long as possible away from Lee.

However, the monotony of camp is broken, about every second day, by portions of our line making reconnaissances and sorties forth on the enemy to feel of him, these generally resulting in pretty lively battles. Day before yesterday we had a very lively fight lasting some 6 or 7 hours and resulting in the capture of an entire South Carolina Regiment. Sheridan manages to out general Early about every time. Why Early lingers so long here I cannot tell. He certainly does not expect to make another invasion as the Potomac River is swimming full from bank to bank and a raid now would be certain destruction to his army.

I hope he may do something soon and relieve our suspense.

It is predicted that we will have active operations soon in this Department. I am already getting tired of lying still and hope it may be so.

I have recd. no letters from home lately, the last being from Uncle William dated at Delaware Sept 5th, though I have written frequently. Tell me whether you ever recd. a large splendid lithographed portrait of Genl. Grant which I sent you per mail Sept. 1st. It is intended to be framed.

The weather is clearing up and getting very fine which I hope may continue so.

Hoping to hear from you soon & often,

I remain Your

Son,

Alex.

The Surprise at Cedar Creek
The Confederate flanking column attacking the 19th Corps from the rear.
Wood Engraving by A. R. Waud

16

Sheridan's Army
Harrisonburg, Rockingham Co.
Va. Sept. 26, 1864

My Dear Parents,

I am again well and blessed with the privilege of writing you again. The last recd. from you was dated Sept 9th.

We have had another glorious victory which is again perched upon our banners. This valley which has always heretofore been the "Valley of Humiliation" has now be come the "Valley of triumph."

We had two terrible & hard fought battles lately, the first at Winchester, Sept. 19th, the other at "Fisher's Hill", near Strasburg, Sept. 22nd, both resulting in the most glorious victory of the war.[39] The particulars, no doubt, you have read are this, in the newspapers. Altogether, we destroyed & captured over ten thousand of the enemy, 29 pieces of artillery, & completely routed him.[40] We have followed up our victory thus far (one hundred & two miles from our base). We came to a halt this morning, and how much further we intend going I am unable to say, perhaps to Richmond.

The General Engagement commenced Monday morning Sept. 19th about daylight, on the Opequon Creek. The 19th and 6th Corps & Torbert's & Averell's cavalry opening out the ball, the lines extending about 7 miles. The battle was hot and stubbornly contested by the enemy until about 2 oclock P.M. when our gallant & daring Corps, under Genl Crook, came up & was ordered to charge, which they did in the most dare devil style. It was the finest thing I have seen during the war. The first day we drove them over 12 miles, fairly strewing the ground for miles & miles, with dead and wounded. We got over 3000 of their wounded gathered into Winchester and they managed to get away with them over 2000 of their wounded.

They afterwards tried in vain to make a stand at "Fisher's Hill" which they always called impregnable, but they could not withstand a flank charge from Crook's Corps which came down on them like an avalanche driving them like sheep. On this "Hill" we took 21 pieces of artillery.[41]

We also killed & Wounded five of their generals. We lost one general killed, Russell of 6th Corps, and three wounded.[42]

But our gallant army of Sheridan, in order to achieve these victories, had to pass through the fiery ordeal of death and carnage, for 'twas five days before we got all our dead buried. They literally lay in piles for miles.

But I cannot write you any particulars but respectfully refer you to the newspapers for minutia.

I have only had 3 minutes to write you this as the mail goes out immediately.

Don't be uneasy about me as I am all O.K.

Truly

Alex

17

Sheridan's Army
Harrisonburg, Va.
Oct. 5th 1864

My Dear Parents,

I again write you from this distant point in "Dixie" letting you know that I am still enjoying good health and prosperity.

Our army has lain here about a week and a half without any more general engagements. Our Cavalry, however, has had several pretty lively fights around in the neighborhood of Staunton and Port Republic, also at the old and ever memorable battlefield of Piedmont.[43]

We are burning and destroying everything in this valley, such as wheat stacks, hay stacks, barns, houses. Indeed, there will be nothing but heaps of ashes and ruins generally between Staunton and Harper's Ferry. Thousands of Refugees are fleeing north daily, as nothing but starvation would stare them in the face to stay in this valley the coming winter. They express themselves as heartily tired of the war and now fully realize that Secession has been a dear thing to them.[44]

Those who have lived before the war in the most affluent and elegant circumstances and in a country the most fertile and beautiful in the world are now reduced to the most abject poverty and beggary. Alas! how the proud and mighty have fallen by this infatuated game of Secession. They are now reaping its rewards.

Lt. Meigs, Engineer on Staff of Genl. Sheridan, & son of Quartermaster General U.S. Army, and an intimate friend of mine, was killed yesterday whilst riding from Genl. Custer's Head Quarters to an outer post.[45] He was a very promising young man, an orderly accompanying him was also killed. The Lieutenant's body was embalmed & will be sent to Washington City, to his family.

My old friend Dr. Gans, Surgeon 10th Va. Inf., died last night from inflammation of the bowels.[46] His body will start back under an escort today. The Doctor was an intimate friend of mine and his loss will be deeply felt among the medical staff of this army. I watched over him to the last, still hoping that he might be saved.

I am now Surgeon in Chief of this 2nd Brigade 1st Div. and a good deal on hand.

I hope this army will soon go back down the valley as I do not think that we will go any further up.

I recd. your letter of the 14th ult., also one from John of 17 ult. Mails are very irregular.

Hoping to hear from you soon & often.

I am yours,

truly

Alex.

18

Sheridan's Army
Strasburg, Va.
Oct. 9th 1864

My Dear Friends,

I again write you letting you know that I am still alive and well.

Our army is lying here at present, having moved back from Harrisonburg the morning of the 6th Oct.

They have followed close on our heels, with how large a force I am unable to say. We had considerable fighting on yesterday afternoon & this forenoon, with what result I am not prepared to say as my Corps was not engaged. We were in the advance & brought to a halt pretty suddenly by the fighting in the rear. As I write, the cannonading has about ceased and the 6th & 19 Corps are resting on Fisher's Hill, some two miles from where I am camped, at the foot of the "Hill" and on the bank of the Shenandoah River.

I think this fighting will amount to nothing of any magnitude, only a few thousand Cavalry.

Last evening I recd. your letter of 23d ult., also at the same time one from Cousin Cyrus & Minnie Richards enclosing her miniature which I now send to you. I also recd. a Gazette & Advocate the other day.

The weather is getting most desperately cold, and I hope we may get back soon to the rear where we can get some clothing & such things, which I think we will do soon.

This Rail Road running to Manassas Junction from here is being opened up & repaired. Stonewall Jackson tore it all to pieces some 3 years since and it has been laying in this condition since.[47]

I wrote you several letters lately, the last from Harisonburg where we lay about eleven days. I trust you have recd. them all.

As Martinsburg is our base now you may as well address my letters there.

Yours Truly

Alex

You can do as you see proper about disposition of that money. Perhaps had better reserve some of it to have access to.

A. N.

Later

An officer has just stepped into my tent & informs me that we captured 5 pieces of artillery & a good many prisoners today in the fight.[48]

Alex

19

Martinsburg, Va.
Oct. 13 1864

My Dear Friends,

Your letter of the 2nd inst was recd. as I came through Winchester the other day & I was glad to hear from you.

My Brigade arrived here last evening coming down from Strasburg to escort a train of supply wagons, also the captured artillery, horses, wagons, & prisoners, that were taken on the 9th inst near Fisher's Hill. There were eleven pieces of artillery & the victory on that day was complete.

On the way down here, we were attacked by Guerrillas, and six of our men killed, 13 wounded & 15 captured, a Colonel & Surgeon on the Staff of Genl. Sheridan were mortally wounded, the doctor since died.[49]

For the outrage, I understand that Genl. Sheridan burned Newtown and all the houses within 5 miles of the place.[50] They attack our trains every day & are a perfect nuisance. I am informed that they kill all the prisoners they take and they have raised the black flag. But there are two sides that can play this game and our boys remember every one they catch, but 'tis best to tell no tales.[51]

I understand that Genl. Crook's Head Quarters will soon be transferred to Cumberland. If this be so, there is perhaps something soft in reserve for us yet.

I presume that we will leave here tomorrow to escort another train back to the front.

John seems to have been very lucky to draw such a prize, but I am really glad he got released.

We were on the march on Election day & consequently many Ohio men in Virginia Regiments did not get to vote, but I see by this mornings paper that Ohio's State ticket went all right.[52]

goodbye,

Alex.

Write to Martinsburg, Va.

20

Winchester, Va.
Sunday Oct. 16, 1864

My Dear Friends,

I again embrace the opportunity of dropping you a line, letting you know that your letter of the 12th inst was received yesterday just before leaving Martinsburg, from which place I wrote you a letter some few days ago. We remained there with our brigade three days & nights, leaving there yesterday for the front to escort another train back. We stopped last night at Bunker Hill, & leaving there this morning, arrived in this City about noon.

Since we left Strasburg, our force had another fight, with what result I know not, only that our good old Brigade Commander Col Geo. Wells 34th Mass. was killed. He was one of the bravest men I ever saw. You have his photograph. How long we will remain at Winchester I am unable to say, perhaps a day or two. Every thing seems lively here under Federal Rule, and the citizens here would gladly remain under this rule here after. They have all had there [sic] fill of secession.

I have just had a good dinner & feel much revived. We have a good many warm friends to the Union cause in this city, though they have been compelled to keep a close mouth most always heretofore.

My health never was better and every one I meet remarks
how fleshy & well I look, notwithstanding the arduous campaign
I have passed through during the past seven months.

I have been clothing myself up from the Wheeling shops &
else where and have about expended my finances, besides what
I am indebted for.

However you need not remit me any thing until I order it.

I have just received a very kind letter from Mrs. Carter, Weston
Mass., in relation to her deceased son about whom I wrote her. I
herewith send you the letter, that you may know they appreciate my kindness.

I am glad that the election passed off so gloriously.

Address me hereafter, until further orders, Martinsburg Va.
as that is our base.

Truly

Alex

21

Sheridan's Army
Hd. Qurs. 2nd Brig 1st Div Army W.Va.
Newtown, Va.
Oct. 21st 1864

My Dear Friends,

I again embrace the opportunity of writing you a line informing you that I am yet alive and well, notwithstanding we passed
through another fiery ordeal on Wednesday Oct. 19th just one
month from the memorable day the battle of Winchester was
fought. It resulted in another brilliant victory to our arms & the
complete rout of the rebel army. This is called the battle of Cedar Creek and was, if possible, more signally triumphant than
any other battle we have fought.

Our Corps (Crook's, generally the 8th) was completely surprised early in the morning, before day light by the rebels capturing our pickets and storming our breastworks, whilst we were
all in bed. They jumped over our works with fixed bayonets,
bayoneting and shooting down our men by the hundreds, before they could get fairly awake. The result was, the whole corps
broke in confusion and to rally them, seemed almost impossible
until they had fled back past the 19th & 6th Corps. A stand here
was made, resulting in one of the hottest battles of the war,
lasting all day from day light until dark, in which the rebel army

was completely routed with great loss. There must have been some four or five thousand killed & wounded altogether.[53]

We captured about sixty pieces of artillery & nearly all their wagon and ambulance train, also took some three or four thousand prisoners.[54]

Early in the morning they took from us some sixteen pieces of artillery and about a thousand prisoners, but the artillery we all re-captured in the afternoon. We lost many brave officers & men in the fight.

Our Division Commander Col Jos. Thoburn, who has been commanding either our brigade or division, all summer, and one of the bravest men who ever lived and who that day fought his twenty fifth battle, was killed. Some few days before that, in my quarters in conversation, he remarked to me that he only wanted to fight one more great battle and then he would be satisfied. I remarked that, that battle might be his last or else give him some little memento that he might show his grand children. He said that was very true, and how true it proved. I can scarcely realize that he is dead, he was so brave, so kind. He was Col. of 1st Va., a physician by profession and Surgeon of same regiment in first 3 months service.

Capt. P. G. Bier, Crook's asst. adjutant General, was mortally wounded & died. He was formerly a Lieutenant in my Regiment and a very efficient officer, and intimate friend of mine, but to mention the names of my friends who fell that day on the battle-field would be unnecessary. So many there were of them.

To go over the battlefield the next day after the battle was a great, but common sight to me, as it was the 10th battle I have been in this summer & fall.

In the confused state of affairs, as occurs after every battle, I am unable to specify details, but refer you to the most accurate newspaper accounts, which no doubt are published ere this.

Little "Phil" is too much for General Early. I think every one must concede.

My brigade came down this morning from Cedar Creek seven miles distant, for the purpose of guarding the "Field Hospitals" which are temporarily established here, but we are shipping the wounded as fast as possible to Winchester some eight miles distant down the valley.[55]

Surgeon Shannon 116th Ohio Regt. was mortally wounded that morning in the panic. He was an intimate friend of mine and an efficient medical officer.

I have not time nor space to write you particulars as I am very busy and hoping you are well.

I remain

Your Son,

Alex.

P.S. Address Martinsburg as usual.

22

Sheridan's Army
Head Quarters 2nd Brig 1st Div.
Army of West Virginia
Newtown, Virginia
October 24th 1864

My Dear Friends,

I am this moment in receipt of your letter of the 17th inst. and very glad to hear of your welfare. Our Brigade is still at Newtown, some seven miles from Cedar Creek, which is the "front". We have been guarding the Hospitals, as I stated to you in a former letter from this place the other day, ever since the great battle of the 19th inst. However we are getting the wounded, both wounded federals and "rebs", shipped away to the rear, as rapidly as is practicable, and after this is completed, then, I presumed we will be relieved at this post and ordered to the front again.

I wrote you the other day the particulars of our great battle of the 19th inst. which I have no doubt you have read all about in the newspapers before this. I hardly think the rebel army will re-organize in the valley again this fall; they have met with so many signal defeats under Early. Indeed, since the 19th of September Sheridan has captured about one hundred pieces of artillery [remainder of page torn and missing] . . . the other day Genl. Sheridan was at Winchester, on his way returning from Washington City and hearing the cannon from afar at the front, jumped onto his Silver saddle, and galloped towards his army, a distance of some fifteen miles. When he arrived, every thing was in a panic and confusion and our troops were then driven as far back as Middletown some 2 or 3 miles and the battle seemed almost lost, but his arrival infused new courage into our soldiers. 'Twas said to be like a reinforcement of twenty thousand men, and when he remarked that "Early should that day get the damndest thrashing, he ever got", and the battle turned to our favor; and such a victory as we had that day I never saw.[56]

I recd. a letter from John today. He was well. Dr. Riddle went to Philadelphia some weeks since to get mustered out of service, together with a number of his regiment whose term had expired.

You speak about an overcoat. I have a government overcoat that I picked up by the way at Lynchburg last June, which does me very well and will answer till I go home which I hope to be able to do as soon as this campaign closes. 'Tis talked . . . strongly that as soon as the . . . [remainder of letter torn and missing].

23

Head Quarters 2nd brig 1st Inf. Div. Army W.Va.
Sheridan's Army
Newtown, Virginia
Oct. 27, 1864

My Dear Friends,

I can again inform you that I am still enjoying good health and prospering finely. My Brigade is still at this town which is some 7 miles from the "Front" but we are expecting to be relieved at this post every day.

Nothing very new has occurred lately hereabouts, except another attack on one of our trains beyond Winchester, on its way up to the "front". The attack was made by a gang of the notorious Mosby's men who succeeded in capturing one of our Genls (Duffie) who is a celebrated cavalry General and has accompanied us through the whole summer campaign. He is a Frenchman, very young, and has been a very different officer, displaying great military genius & bravery in the different engagements this Summer.[57]

Every thing seems quiet at the front now days and I hardly think the rebels in the valley will risk another battle this fall, but if they do, I am confident that little "Phil Sheridan" is ready for them.

My Head Quarters are in an old mansion formerly owned by Lord Fairfax. Indeed, this celebrated old Lord, once owned all the country for many miles around here and in early days with gun and hounds, chased the deer over these hills and vallies, once considered so sacred, now rendered so memorable from the many sanguinary engagements fought on the soil, beneath which repose the bodies of so many of our gallant dead, for it seems one continuous sepulcher from the Potomac to Lynchburg.

But I have not time to theorize, or I might write many interesting things.

I have been invited to tea this Evening with a beautiful young Southerner, a daughter of an aged brother disciple of the healing art, with whom I have many pleasant talks. He is a graduate of the University of Pennsylvania of the class of 1820, and has grown grey in his profession. During this long period of arduous professional duties, he tells me, he has never been physically disqualified a single day from attending to these duties.

I must close hoping to hear from you soon.

I am Yours

Most Sincerely

Alex.

24

Newtown, Va.
Nov. 2nd 1864

My Dear Friends,

I again write you letting you know that I am still well and at the same place from which I last wrote you.

I receive today your letter of Oct. 24th, also one of the July 20th which had gone astray somewhere, along with a great many others for our Regiment. This old letter had enclosed, clippings from the Del. Gazette, about Commencement exercises which were quite interesting to me.

I am glad to hear of your welfare, but sorry that you have so much trouble with James.

I must advise you, by all means, to send him to the Infirmary, if he causes you so much trouble. There certainly could be no reflections by any one about it as all know the necessity which has driven you to it. For my own part, I advise this step.

You ask me about the propriety of sending Mrs. Carter that letter. You can do as you like about this, but the sight of it might possibly make her feel still worse.

I wrote to her that the grave of her son was marked, that he was buried with a good many others, near our Field Hospital on the Opequon Creek some 5 miles from the City of Winchester, that it was impractical at present to obtain his body on account of the Guerrillas infesting that particular locality, there being no direct communication at present, by pike, between Winchester and Harper's Ferry, between which two places he is buried.

I advised her to take no steps towards getting it until affairs were a little more settled in the valley. His watch, money &c. I never saw, but suppose he was robbed by the rebels on the field when they advanced over it, as they make a practice of stripping our dead & wounded of every thing, even their clothes.

Well, I have nothing very new to write, as the army still lays on Cedar Creek, and the enemy, I believe, no nearer than New Market, and I think there is no probability of another engagement very soon, though it is reported that they have been reinforced pretty heavily since the battle. My Brigade is still at this town, occupying it as kind of an outpost.

It is a great rebel town; however I have been out at several tea parties lately and am treated very respectfully by the ladies particularly. We have quite a number of rebel wounded here to look after, all who were able to bear transportation having been sent to Winchester.

The mail is going. I hope to get home by Christmas at least.

Write soon

Alex.

25

Sheridan's Army
2nd Brig. 1st Inf. Div.
Army West Virginia
Middle Military Division
Newtown, Virginia
Novr. 4th, 1864

My Dear Friends,

I again write you from the same point in "Dixie", letting you know that I am still very well and prospering finely.

Nothing particularly startling has transpired, since my last, in this Department. The enemy are reported as being in the neighborhood of New Market and heavily reinforced since the last battle. I do not know how reliable this report may be.

The weather is beginning to assume rather a wintry aspect, and pretty rough for soldiering. I have been favored very much since being at Newtown, in having a house for head quarters, but do not know how soon I shall have to take to the ground again.

I have been invited out to several dinner & tea parties of late here and am treated very well by both Secesh & Union, of the latter class there are however but precious few.

We have to care for quite a number of rebel wounded, who being unable to bear transportation to the rear, were left in this town. They are some of the worst cases, among these is a rebel Major Clyburne of 2nd South Carolina Infantry Regt. who is lying at a private house. He is but a mere youth in appearance, very gentlemanly in his manners and very courteous.

He has been in the army about four years and in different battles has been wounded nine times, the last time in the battle of Cedar Creek Oct 19th in which he lost his left leg.

He is from the "hot bed of Secession", Charleston S.C. and has been reared in the first of Southern Society. He is a brave boy and his gallantry is worthy of a nobler cause. I give him the same care that I give my own men, remembering the injunction "Love Your Enemies, do good to those who hate you &c." and in doing this I lose nothing.

I hope to be able to get home by Christmas, at least, and make all my friends a visit.

Hoping to hear from you soon, I am

Your, most Sincerely,

Alex.

26

Newtown, Virginia
Novr. 7th, 1864

My Dear Friends,

Your letter of the 31st ult. was recd. on yesterday, containing an account of mother's sickness. I am very sorry to hear of this and sincerely hope that it may be nothing serious. I am not at all surprised to hear of her being sick as I know she has worked and worried herself almost to death about James who ought to have been sent to the Infirmary long ago. It is nothing but justice to do such a thing and certainly no one could think hard of it as Every body knows full well the state of affairs. I hope in your next letter to hear of mother's recovery and of your having sent James away.

Nothing very new has occurred in this Department lately.

The Guerrillas under Mosby are very troublesome, murdering some of our men every day, almost in sight of town. It would be a great blessing to rid the Country of this terrible land pirate. We string his men up whenever caught, but still they hover around, murdering & robbing.

I am in great hurry and must close. I am quite well.

Hoping to hear from you soon,

I am yours truly,

Alex

27

Sheridan's Army
Newtown, Va.
Tuesday Morning
Novr. 9th, 1864

My Dear Friends,

I again embrace the opportunity of writing you a line letting you know that I am very well and enjoying life finely. I feel very solicitous about mother's welfare and sincerely hope that she is better before this time.

I hope to be able to see you all against Christmas, as there will be no possible chance of getting a "leave" before that time, I think. According to a recent order, no deduction is made from officer's pay during leave of absence as formerly, which is a very good thing.

We have all been packed up and readvised yesterday and ordered "to be on the alert and ready to move at a moment's notice, either up or down the valley." We are ready for an attack at any moment. 'Tis reported that the rebel Genl. Rosser, with about 5000 cavalry & 2 Batteries, has gone around on the other side of North Mountain towards Cumberland on a raiding expedition, and that Genl. Custer is after him with a sufficient force to take him properly in hand.[58]

Our Brigade is in line of battle every morning at 4 o'clock, remaining so until day-light. 'Tis necessary to be on the alert, as we are liable to be captured any morning, our little force being in an exposed position off from the main army.

Yesterday was the great election day which I suppose elected old Abe again. I suppose you had lively times in the United States. In the Confederacy it was a very rainy, blue devil day.

I must close hoping to hear that mother is better, the next word.

I am Yours,

Most Sincerely,

Alex.

28

From Sheridan's Army
In the Field
4 miles south of Winchester
Sunday Novr. 13th, 1864

My Dear Friends,

Our army moved from Cedar Creek to this place on the 9th & 10 inst. My Brigade also moved from Newtown on the evening of the 10th inst. and joined the main army here.

The Enemy has followed pretty closely on our heels and engaged our cavalry every day since the 9th, no general engagement however. Last night was a bright cold frosty moonlight night and the fighting was kept up until after midnight, in which we charged them capturing over 300 prisoners. 'Tis said that Early has gone to Richmond, having been superseded by Ewell and that his Army has been heavily reinforced since the battle of the 19th ult.

We have thrown up a line of earthworks at this place, reaching in length some 8 or 10 miles, somewhat shaped like a letter V, our Corps (the Army of West Virginia, sometimes called the 8th) occupying the extreme left.

'Twas thought yesterday that a great battle would come off to-day, seeing that it was Sunday, but every thing seems very quiet to-day, all along the lines, except an occasional crack of a carbine from the videttes at the outer picket posts.

The weather is getting most terribly cold and very unpleasant in camp, as we have nothing but small flies, open at both ends and no chance for fire, to use as a tabernacle.

I am writing this in a house close by where I have slept two nights lately.

I am hoping that we will soon get permanently established in Winter quarters, and get fixed up as this is a very hard way of living in cold weather.

I have not recd. any letters from home lately, not since I was informed of mother's illness and am somewhat uneasy about hearing from her. I sincerely hope that she is better before this time.

I enclose you a beautiful poem on the death of Col. Thoburn, published in the Baltimore American.[59]

To know the lamented Thoburn was but to love him. He was our Brigade Commander for a long time and then afterwards our Division Commander and no braver man then he ever carried a sword.

When the war first broke out in the Spring of '61, he was practicing medicine in the City of Wheeling, and was Commissioned Surgeon of the 1st Va. Infy, then commanded by Col. Kelley (now Maj. Genl. Kelley). Having served his 3 months in the capacity of Surgeon, he was commissioned Col. of the Regiment for the 3 years service, and when he was killed at Cedar Creek the 19th Oct. he only had about 5 days to serve until his time would expire. He fought that day his 25th battle, covering himself all over in glory. He had been time and again offered a brigade generalship, but refused. Many score of times he has come in and visited me at my head quarters and chatted the hours away.

Long will the memory of Thoburn be cherished dear in the hearts of the soldiers from West Virginia.

Hoping to hear from you soon and to hear of mother being better.

I close by remaining,

Your Affectionate Son,

Alex.

29

Sheridan's Army
4 miles South Winchester, Va.
In the Field
Novr. 19th, 1864

My Dear Friends at Home,

I again write you informing you of my welfare and prosperity away in "Dixie".

It has now been nearly one week since I heard from home and I now begin to feel quite uneasy about mother's condition, however, I am in hope of hearing soon again of her recovery.

Nothing very strange has occurred here in our army since my last letter to you, and I think now that there is not much prospect of any more fighting here, for a while, at least.

It is thought that a portion of our army will, perhaps, go into Winter quarters at this place, but I hardly think that the whole army will.

It is sincerely hoped that Crook's Corps will be sent back to their old places along the Rail Road and to the Kanawaha region.

Still it is very uncertain what disposition will be made of us.

We may form a junction or co-operate with Sherman. May assist in capturing Wilmington, or may knock with Grant at the door of Richmond before another Spring.

We can make no calculations for the future.
Everything is very high in the way of living,
Bread $1.00 per small loaf
Butter .75 cts a piece
Pies (small) 50 cts a piece
Cheese 50 cts per pound
Ham 30 cts per pound
Coffee 60 per pound
Sugar 25 per pound
Potatoes 2.50 per bushel
    &c. &c.
and every thing from Sutlers at deathly prices, but we are compelled to stand it.

However our salaries are raised considerably, to commence the first of November.

I must close,

Hoping to hear from you soon

Alex.

31

From Sheridan's Army
Camp Russell
4 Miles south Winchester
Novr. 21, 1864

My Dear Friends,

I am in receipt today of your letter of the 15th inst. containing the intelligence that mother was convalescing.

This I am very much gratified to learn, as I feared she might not have the strength to rally from a spell of fever.

I am also very glad to know that you have got James transferred to the Infirmary as I never felt easy when I thought of him being at home and him so dangerous at times. I hope he may stay there the remainder of his days.

Nothing very new has occurred here in this Department lately; only the most reliable intelligence informs us that Early's army left Strasburg, a day or two since, for Staunton and they have abandoned the great Valley of Virginia to the "Yankee Vandals."

About fifteen thousand of our cavalry started this morning, up the valley, on a small reconnaissance after the Johnnies, to learn the truth of their where abouts. The Johnnies about one week ago, thinking that two of our Army Corps had gone to

Richmond, came down and pitched into Powell's division, getting beautifully thrashed, losing about 200 prisoners, 2 cannon and 2 Battleflags. They then "went for" our cavalry under Merritt and Custer and the ragged devils were driven through Newtown south with so much celerity that one could play marbles on their coat tails.

They thus ascertained that the Corps under Emory and Wright were still here under "little Phil" and wisely concluded that "discretion was the better part of valor" and "he that fights and runs away would live to fight another day," and I am really glad if they have gone, which deserters to our army report to be the case. Then should this be true, I think it all together probable that it will materially change the aspect of affairs in this Sector and that our army here, will not all remain here very long. However Winchester will be held the coming winter as the Rail Road to that city from Harper's Ferry is about finished. It is called the Winchester and Potomac R.R. and has been all torn to pieces during the last 3 years, but will soon make Winchester our great base of supplies, instead of Martinsburg.

We had been working lately at the Manassas gap and Strasburg old road, repairing it, laying track &c. &c. and had repaired it as far as Front Royal, but I learn now that Sheridan has abandoned the project and is removing the iron thus laid to the Winchester & Potomac R.R.[60]

The rainy season seems to be fully inaugurated here in the valley, making every thing very disagreeable.

I received another letter from Mrs. Carter, Mass., which I enclose to you. I have just answered it, giving her all the desired information.

Hoping to hear from you soon, I am yours truly,

Alex.

32

From 2nd Brig. lst Infy Div. Army West Va.
Middle Military Division
Stephenson's Depot Frederick Co., Va.
Winchester & Potomac Rail Road
November 25th, 1864

My Dear Friends at Home,

Our Brigade marched from Camp Russell, our last camp, yesterday, to this Depot, which is now the terminus of the Winchester & Potomac R.R. It has been repaired this far for a few days, and whether the design is, to repair the road as far as Winchester, some five miles farther south, I am unable to say at present.

I presume that it is intended for our brigade to do guard duty here, for a while at least, there is another brigade of our division, stationed at Summit Point, the next depot towards Harper's Ferry. It is the memorable station that we marched out from on the 19th day of September, to give battle to Genl Early, which resulted in a conflict so glorious to our arms. It sounds so natural to hear the old locomotives, this morning, whistling fine music, as they come in pulling long trains, groaning with their load of provisions for Sheridan's grand army; and to hear the click of hammers an pikes, laying side track and switches.

Myself and Chaplain are occupying a room in the old Stephenson Mansion, it being the most beautiful place I have seen in the Great Valley of Virginia. This splendid house and elegant surrounding might, one day, have been the fit habitation for a King, but alas the sad, desolating and destructive hand of war, has made sad work among the beautiful evergreens, shaded avenues and summer bowers that once made this estate almost a perfect paradise.

Since the war began, the proud and once noble rich Stephenson family has been scattered and many changes have been wrought in the family circle. The father, first died, then afterwards the mother; then a son; afterwards a beautiful daughter; leaving only two daughters with about fifty servants to occupy the once happy house, and these servants troubled with freedom "on the brain" and with the north star for their guide, one after another started out, until they were all gone in quest of that "happy land of Canan." And lastly, the two beautiful daughters, bid farewell to the dear old mansion about two weeks since going to Berryville Clarke Co. Va. to make their future home.[61]

A widow woman now occupies a portion of the house, and has kindly given the Chaplain and myself a beautiful front room, in which to have our headquarters.

The last letter received from home was of the 15th inst. I hope that the next letter I get from home will inform me of mother's recovery.

Yesterday was the great national thanksgiving day and Sheridan's Army was the recipient of forty thousand pounds of turkey and chicken for a great dinner. These were contributed by the good people residing in the Eastern cities. The soldiers were very thankful and consider this as an appreciation, by the good people at home, of their labors in the valley.

I must close by hoping to hear from you soon,

And Remaining,

Yours Sincerely,

Alex.

33

Stephenson's Mansion
Stephenson's Depot
Frederick Co., Va.
Decr. 1st, 1864

My Dear Friends at Home,

I am in receipt of your favor of the 21st ult, also copies of Gazette & Advocate, all of which I was very glad to receive, particularly to learn that mother was recovering. I hope that she may get along now without any relapse.

I also recd. a letter from John yesterday, dated Nov. 17th. I had just written to him the day before. He spoke of Sattie being sick but getting better at that time.

My Brigade is still stationed at this Depot which is now getting to be a very lively place. It having become now the great base of Supplies for Sheridan's Army, instead of Martinsburg, the last wagon train coming from Martinsburg yesterday, that will come.

I suppose that a Post office will soon be established here for the army as they began yesterday to run regular passenger trains on this road, to connect with trains on the Baltimore & Ohio R.R. at Harper's Ferry.

The weather here is most delightful, the sun shinning like in Spring, as though winter had forgotten to make its appearance. I hope it may continue so many weeks.

I see that the rebels have made another dash on the B.& O. R.R. at New Creek & Piedmont, capturing the garrison and destroying things very generally. There were some fifteen hundred of them under Rosser and McCausland, but as our gallant Custer is after them, I think they will not make much by the operation.[62]

I was in hope that we would have got back on the B. & O. R.R. before this as we had been promised it some time ago by Genl. Crook, but I suppose we are doomed to wait a while longer.

We are watching the papers very closely now days for Sherman, earnestly praying that this boldest movement of the war may be crowned with success. The Richmond papers are now perfectly reticent in regard to his movements, thinking the Yankees in the north may look elsewhere for information.

I am now almost beginning to get homesick as nearly a year has elapsed since my visit home, but as it is now, I have no prospects yet awhile for a leave, as none are granted now days.

From the best & most reliable information, Early seems not to have left the valley yet but continues to hover around "Rude Hill" between Mt. Jackson & New Market, watching "little Phil" with a hawk's eye and the watching seems to be mutual on the part of both.

I think however that Early will soon either play out or starve out as we destroyed every thing in the shape of sustenance between Staunton and this point; but the rebel army seems to live on nothing. I am confident that if our men were as hard up as they are, that they would all desert and go home.

Well, well, I sincerely hope to get home sometime this winter and make you a good visit.

You speak about Miss Josephine Atkinson living at our house. It strikes me very forcibly that I am acquainted with Miss Atkinson and that she is a very pretty girl, if I know her, just give her my kind regards.

I find, existing here in this neighborhood, quite a Union Sentiment among the inhabitants, many of whom who were rabid secessionists early in the war and some of whom who were really in the rebel army, have renounced their allegiance to the so called Southern Confederacy and have returned like the prodigal very repentant. They begin to see the folly of the thing and to realize that Secession has been a very dear thing to them.

Address me not as before but to Stephenson's Depot Va. via Harper's Ferry Va.

Hoping to hear from you soon

I am yours truly,

Alex.

34

Stephenson's Depot, Va.
Dec. 6th 1864

My Dear Friends,

I again write you informing you that I am still here in the same place and prospering very finely.

Nothing very strange or startling has transpired in this Department since my last letter to you the other day, except some of our army has been transferred to Grant, two divisions of the 6th Army Corps having gone already and the other division will soon follow. I think the 19th Corps is destined to winter in the valley and also probably our Corps, though about the latter it is uncertain.

To-day's paper reports good things from Sherman about whom we have been so solicitous for so long. He seems to be driving a wholesale business down about the seaboard about this time, whilst Thomas is managing things beautifully in the neighborhood of Nashville.[63]

Everything seems to be working gloriously towards the advance of our cause, and I doubt not that in a few months hence a new phase of things will appear.

The Southern Confederacy has now dwindled down to a mere shell and I think is destined to go under before many months.

The weather here still continues most beautiful and the health of the command most excellent.

I should like very much to go home now but I have no prospect of getting a leave of absence for some time yet.

I enclose you a rough miniature of the undersigned which was taken in the field.

Hoping to hear from you soon and often

I close,

Address,

Stephenson's Depot, Va.

via Harper's Ferry, Va.

Truly Yours, Alex.

35

Stephenson's Depot, Va.
Thursday Eve. Dec. 8th, 1864

My Dear Father & Mother,

I again embrace the opportunity of dropping you another line informing you of the receipt of mother's letter of Decr. 1st this evening. You may rest assured I was very glad to learn that mother had so far recovered as to be able to write me a letter in her own hand. I have been very uneasy about her; but now I feel that she will get along should she meet with no back set.

The weather has changed in the last day to be very cold, old winter having been inaugurated in good earnest. I rode up to Winchester & returned this afternoon. 'Twas very cold riding. I have a great many good Union friends upon whom I call quite often in Winchester, also there are many there, of quite warm Southern feelings, who are very good friends of mine.

My memory of Winchester and of many of her inhabitants will ever be of a most pleasant character. It was here that George Washington spent many of his palmiest days, and during the Revolution constructed here a Fort of some magnitude,[64] the remains of which are standing to this day. He also dug here a well one hundred and three feet in depth, in which there is this day some sixty feet of water, out of which, the soldiers quartered in Winchester, get their water. The place is also rendered historic as being the burial place of Lord Fairfax[65] and Major Gen. Daniel Morgan, who was one of the greatest and bravest generals of the Revolutionary war.

I wrote you a day or two since. Nothing very strange has occurred lately hereabouts, all seeming quiet in the front.

At present I can give you no definite information about when you might look for me home, only this winter some time anyhow.

I may possibly go by way of New Castle Pa. and take Minnie along with me. This will depend on how long a leave of absence I may get. Joe and Ella seem to know more about my matrimonial prospects than I do myself.

My love to all,

truly yours,

Alex

36

Stephenson's Depot, Va.
December 15th, 1864

My Dear Friends at Home,

Your letter written this 6th inst. was recd. this morning; also this evening recd. two newspapers, Gazette & Advocate; the letter enclosed some postage stamps, for all of which favors I thank you. We are still stationed at the same Depot and probably destined for the winter here. No very particular changes have occurred here in our army since my last. I believe, except that all of the Sixth Army Corps have left us and either gone to Sherman or Grant.

It is universally acknowledged to be the best fighting Corps in the whole army and we are very loath to part with it. We still have a large army in the Valley which will in all probability spend the winter here. Genl. Sheridan has his head quarters in Winchester, and the greater portion of the army lies some four miles beyond town towards Strasburg and Front Royal. Genl. Early, it is reported, has his headquarters at New Market, but a very large part of his army has been sent to Richmond and I am rather inclined to think that he will make no further demonstrations against our lines this winter again.[66]

My brigade is doing first rate here at the great base of supplies and living on the fat of the land. The men have very comfortable winter quarters erected and I think will be very well satisfied to remain here all winter. I find a great Union Sentiment prevailing in this section of the Valley and have many invitations all around to enjoy their hospitality. I have visited some friend every day for the past week and have enjoyed these visits very much. I and "Charlie" have just returned this evening from a half day's visit to Dr. Cochran's house some 2 miles away. These Union people are truly martyrs and have reason to be praised. Dr. Cochran's house is all marked with bullets and every door has been fired through by rebel assassins who sought his life. He has been imprisoned and has suffered every thing but death from the rebel's hands rather than renounce his principles and become a traitor to his Country. He has two sons in our army. His is but one of many similar cases in the Valley that I might relate. But thanks to our gallant army, a brighter day is about dawning, and the beautiful Valley of Virginia, redeemed, regenerated and disinthralled [sic], will no longer be called the 'dark Valley of the shadow of death," but baptized in the blood of a score of battles, will return to her allegiance, humbler and purer than before.

Yesterday I dined, with some of Genl. Emorys staff of 19th Corps, at the palatial mansion of Mr. Jollieffe[67] who is one of the staunch loyal men of Frederick County. Genl. Breckinridge, some weeks since, made his head quarters at his house, and Early's army destroyed every thing he had, but his home.

I recd. a letter yesterday from Cousin Cyrus and Minnie. I wrote them that I wanted Minnie ready and that I would go that way some time this winter and take her home with me. 'Twill not be a great deal out of my way.

I have not heard anything concerning Uncle William and family lately, but suppose they are still on the old farm. I am sorry that he failed to get the Klapp farm in Berlin. Perhaps you might get him another farm in the county that would suit him equally well.

I think I may be safe in predicting that I shall visit home sometime during the month of January, perhaps the latter part of the month. You see they only allow so many medical officers absent from the Corps at a time, and I think my turn will come in about one month or so. I am pretty homesick but hope to see you all this winter.

I am very glad that mother is recovering so and hope she will try and take care of herself when she does get up. My love to all enquiring friends and hoping to hear from you soon.

I am Yours,

Respectfully,

Alex.

37

Stephenson's Depot, Virginia
Saturday Evening Decr. 17th, 1864

My Dear Father & Mother,

Your letter of the 12th Decr. was laid on my table this evening an I now hasten to reply. However I wrote you, but day before yesterday.

After reading your letter to Aunt Lydia and Lizzie's reply to the same, I have concluded not to go by way of New Castle when I go home, unless they should write a more satisfactory letter in the meanwhile.

You have received my letter enclosing my miniature and want to know (as a matter of course) what I wore and all about it. I had on my velvet Cavalry Jacket covered with gold-lace, but no shoulder straps; also my velvet pants with the usual amount of gold lace to which a staff officer is entitled. That's all. That's all mother except my shirt.

I have returned this evening from the country about Brucetown and Jordan's Spring, whither I had gone to visit a sick safeguard from our command and also to call on some of my loyal friends of Frederick County.

I visited and took tea at the house of Mr. Lanquary, a brother of our old friend, William Lanquary of Champaign Co. Ohio. He has a daughter who is very much like her Cousin Emma in Ohio. I told them all about their friends in Ohio of whom they were glad to hear. He is a "well-to-do" farmer, although he has suffered very much from the different armies. He is running a pretty extensive grist mill at present. He is one of the few faithful and loyal men of this country.

A note has just been brought in by my orderly and laid on the table; it is from Dr. Housten, a Citizen Physician some two miles away, who solicits a consultation with me tomorrow at 9 o'c'k A.M. with reference to the case of a sick lady, the wife of a Citizen by the name of Ambrose. I am also invited to dine with the Doctor at 2 oclock P.M.

A hundred guns were fired yesterday at Sheridans headquarters in honor of Genl. Thomas' recent victory,[68] also another hundred this afternoon in honor of Sherman in Savannah.

I'll try and see you in about one month, if Providence and the General permit.

From what I can ascertain from Company D; Uncle William Neil is still residing on the same old farm at Valley Grove, though he sold it some months since for 50.-$ per acre to Messrs Chamber & Davis, to hold possession until April I believe.

I must close by hoping to hear from you soon,

I am dear friends

Your most Sincerely

Alexr.

P.S. Sunday Evening Decr. 18th, 1864

We have just received order to be in readiness at 9. o'clock tomorrow morning to move by rail.

There are good many surmises and rumors as regards our destination. Some say, Petersburg, others Saltwater, and West Virginia, but I think the most reliable is that our Brigade is going to Cumberland Md. which will suit the undersigned "muchly." I think that nothing but our Division, Commanded by Genl. Harris,[69] will move. Good night. I'll write you again.

Alex.

Epilogue

"'Twas the proudest day of my life."
December 21, 1864–June 22, 1865

With little fear of the resurgence of a military threat in the Shenandoah Valley, Grant shifted a number of units from Sheridan's army to augment his forces around Petersburg and Richmond. On December 19 Neil and the veterans of the 12th West Virginia boarded a train at Stephenson's Depot and departed for Washington where they then embarked on a steamer headed for City Point. Stopping briefly there, they continued up to Bermuda Hundred, only to transfer to another ship which carried them to Chaffin's Farm. The West Virginians, now attached to the XXIV Corps under the command of Major General Edward O. C. Ord of the Army of the James, occupied the extreme right, near the Dutch Gap Canal. Apprehensive, they were far from pleased with their new assignment. Neil lamented, "Our boys are very much worried about this thing of being put in the Slaughter pens around Richmond, after all the hardships and battles they have undergone during the past campaign. It does seem very hard."[1]

Neil and the West Virginians, despite continuous Confederate shelling of the canal, lived comfortably in the log cabins temporarily vacated by a division of General Benjamin Butler's Army of the James, then on an expedition against Wilmington. But on their return the West Virginians were moved some five miles on the right flank where the pioneer corps constructed cabins for them. A pleased Neil on January 4 reported to his family, "Tomorrow, I shall have a

93

lot of beautiful pines and cedars planted in front of my house and festoons of evergreens hung around my door to present an air of neatness and cheerfulness."[2] An even more pleasant respite for Neil came later in the month, when he received a leave of absence to visit his family in Ohio. By the middle of February he was again with his regiment "lying immediately at the front breastworks and within speaking distance of the rebel army."[3]

Life at the front for the West Virginians, despite Southern bombardments, bore the tedium of a siege. Fortunately, Neil occasionally secured a Richmond newspaper from the videttes to read. Constant reviews also served to occupy their time. "The Commanding General," as Neil informed his family, "seems to have 'reviews on the brain.' But this constitutes part of the 'pomp & circumstance of war' and I suppose is all right." Later in commenting on their frequency and with perceptive insight Neil added, "I think they are the grandest thing connected with a military life, and are calculated to stimulate the soldier and promote a pride and good feeling in every one." Another obvious diversion for the regiment was the frequent executions "in front of my head-quarters about every day. Day before yesterday 3 men were hung for murder & robbery. 'Tis a very common sight that one gets used to very soon."[4]

The influx of deserters also broke the monotony. It provided the Federals with important intelligence of the deteriorating Confederate morale. News of Southern reverses and Grant's order promising amnesty accelerated the desertion of disillusioned Confederates. Neil noted that "Our boys on picket have circulated among them a good many copies of this order."[5] By early March the perception of an impending Confederate collapse kindled an anticipation among the West Virginians of a pending attack against Southern lines. Neil reported to his family, "Our Division has been under marching orders for more than a week, all packed up & ready. We would not be surprised at any time to see Petersburg and Richmond evacuated." Eight days later a more somber Neil wrote, "Every thing here appears ominous of a big battle soon, which will make a terrible slaughter. Their works are very formidable and they continue to strengthen them every day." On March 27 the waiting finally ended for the West Virginians. Anticipation suddenly became a reality. The XXIV Corps, with the collapse of the Southern lines around Petersburg and the retreat of the Army of Northern Virginia westward, moved quickly. Hurriedly the corps moved along the South Side Railroad in pursuit of Lee. An exhilarated Neil, writing to his parents on April 1, exclaimed, "We are still gaining ground hallelujah! I am writing this on the head of a drum, in the field whilst there is heavy cannonading & musketry all around me. The bullets go 'Spat' every minute near me on all sides. I am right behind a line of works & pretty safe, though there is not much safety anywhere, as the fighting is all around."[6] The chase finally ended at Appomattox Court House. There on April 9, 1865, the Army of Northern Virginia laid down its arms, and Lee surrendered to General Ulysses S. Grant. For Neil, "'Twas the proudest day of my life."[7]

With the war over in Virginia and the surrender of General Joseph Johnston to General William Tecumseh Sherman on April 26 near Durham Station, North Carolina, the veteran West Virginians anticipated "that we will, most of us, be mustered out of service before very long."[8] However, one last assignment awaited the regiment. It served temporarily as part of the army of occupation in Richmond, while Governor Francis Pierpont reconstituted civil authority.[9] On April 25 the XXIV Army Corps entered the fallen Confederate capital. A proud Neil, writing to his parents, wrote, "our [XXIV] corps entering the City with all the 'pomp and circumstance of war' with bands playing and banners flaunting, the latter all draped in mourning for our late President.[10] All officers wear crape on the left arm for six months in token respect. We paraded the principal streets & avenues of the city and were gazed upon by thousands."[11]

In Richmond Neil, somewhat surprised, found that former Confederate officers and citizens eagerly sought the restoration of peace. As he observed, "Business here is beginning to open up pretty lively and the thorough-fares are crowded with people, all seeming very well satisfied with the hope of a speedy termination of the war on 'any kind of terms.'"[12] The respite there did allow Neil and his compatriots an opportunity for sightseeing. Relishing the relaxation, he visited all the points of historical interest and those made infamous by the war, such as Libby Prison and Belle Island. As he noted in writing home, "Our army here is enjoying what we call 'Sunday Soldiering' or 'Soft Soldiering', which is nothing more than we deserve after our many hardships and sufferings." For Neil, Richmond "'tis one of the most beautiful Cities I have ever stopped in."[13]

Thoughts about re-entering civilian life also began to consume considerable attention for Neil's comrades. The idea of "'emigrating' to Mexico" caused "great excitement" in his regiment. Neil considered that possibility, for as he wrote, "Nothing like enterprise and expeditions." But as the day for his regiment to be mustered out of service approached, he gave thought to another possibility, a medical commission "in a new regiment, and should there not be too heavy a rush I may get the Surgeoncy or Asst. Surgeoncy." He shrewdly noted, "some of the officers are not so particularly desirous of quitting the drippings of Uncle Sam's Treasury, for although we do a credit business with him, he is a very responsible functionary and always liquidates his debts to the satisfaction of all parties with whom he has dealings." Yet Neil believed that he had a "very good" chance of getting a commission. He also noted a change in his attitude towards the military, "I am now soldiering for money not Country; for the latter I have already done enough."[14] None of the options materialized, and Neil soon prepared to return home along with the other veterans of his regiment.

Formal proceedings and the weather delayed his regiment's departure from Richmond. An exasperated Neil informed his family that "we are still here and cannot get away unti the Corps has another grand Review at which some medals are to be presented to gallant & meritorious soldiers." Rain temporarily forced the review's postponement. At last, on June 13, despite the weather, the corps paraded. Three days later Neil's regiment was mustered out in Richmond. Only a final journey to Wheeling remained for the 12th West Virginia Regiment. There they received their last payment, and the citizens of Wheeling gratefully honored the regiment with a public celebration.[15]   .

Appendix A

"Lee's Surrender"

Appomattox C.H. Va.
April 10th, 1865

My Dear People,

I am very well & am now permitted to write you a line, for the first time since Apr. 1st.

To record the mighty events that have transpired in this army during the past week or two would require a pen to run more freely than mine, and as I cannot do justice to the subject, I shall be very brief. My command was in the four days battle before Petersburg Mch 30-31, Aprl. 1 & 2, the last day charging and taking several strong forts, the last greatest of which was Fort Gregg, on whose parapet the tattered old banner of the 12th Va. was the first to be planted; three color bearers were shot down before it was planted. The struggle was desperate & our loss of course very heavy. On the morning of April 3d, our good old stars & stripes floated over Richmond & Petersburg, Lee evacuating, the night previous.

We then moved on after Lee fighting him day & night & capturing prisoners by the tens of thousands, following down the South Side Rail Road & branching off towards Lynchburg at Burkesville we followed the branch, marching in some six columns, embracing a width of some thirty miles, sweeping every thing before us until we got within 25 miles of Lynchburg, at this place,

Appomattox C.H. We fought him here & drove him from the field. The great General was in a dilemma, his communications all cut, surrounded by over a hundred thousand soldiers, flushed with success; his supplies exhausted, his army disheartened; he put up the white flag about 10 o'clock a.m. yesterday. The firing then ceased on both sides and the two grand armies lay in full view of each other not over half a mile a part. The spectacle was grand, no tongue can tell, no pen describes the joy that came from the lips of all. 'Twas the proudest day of my life. I am proud of belonging to the 24th Corps, for 'twas by the forced marching day & night that Lee's retreat was cut off & 'twas immediately in front of this corps that the might Army of Northern Virginia surrendered. When Genl. Ord announced that the last battle had been fought, the shouts that went up from our army fairly rent the heavens. The men threw their hats in the air and fairly wept with joy. The shouts were even taken up by the rebel army and loud & long was the cheering. The Bands of both armies played national pieces & everybody was so happy he knew not what to do. The victory was so great we could not realize it, to think of this four years of bloodshed & sacrifice and to think of its close. The rebel army was even more rejoiced than we, & the two thousand prisoners of our's that they had with them even cried with joy when they knew they had been delivered. They came over last night.

I was at the House in Appomattox when Genl. Lee & our Generals had the conference. I saw the great Lee. His head is white as snow, about 60 yrs of age & dressed in fine grey with a white hat & feather, rides an iron grey horse. He is a handsome man and looks like a Statesman. Poor Robert, had to be humiliated; still we recognize him as a great general.

His army at the present writing still lays where it did when it surrendered and has not come over yet, but will some time to day. We have not been permitted to mingle together yet. This ever memorable Appomattox C.H. will live in history as long as time lasts & no doubt a picture of this scene will be seen in Harper & Leslie in less than two weeks & doubtless will be engraved in steel ere long. Our sacrifices have been great and our marches & fighting most terrible lately, but we are now fully compensated for all.

I feel too happy to write anything sensible & lengthy and I must close. I don't know when I can mail this nor whether one will go from here. We have recd. no mail since we left Petersburg.

Good Bye

Your Son

Alex

P.S! I enclose a sprig of cedar plucked from a tree in the yard of Major McLean Appomattox C.H. at whose house the capitulation between Genls Lee & Grant took place on the 9th inst. It will be a relic in years to come.

Endnotes

PREFACE

1. Alexander Neil to Father and Mother, July 23, 1863, Alexander Neil Papers, University of Virginia, Charlottesville, Virginia.

    The assistant surgeon of the 12th West Virginia was then a prisoner of war in Richmond, but "when exchanged would return to his Regt. So I could but accept. . . ." However, he was to remain with the regiment for the remainder of the war.

    Wheeling, a city on the Ohio River in the western panhandle of Virginia with a population of 14,083 in 1860, was the temporary capital of the new state of West Virginia. In the Virginia secession convention at Richmond 32 delegates out of 47 from the western section opposed the ordinance. Unionists in the region quickly undertook a movement for the creation of a new state. After thirteen months of political activity, maneuvering in Congress, approval of a statehood measure by Lincoln, and finally a referendum on the constitution, the president declared West Virginia's admission as a state on June 20, 1863. See Charles H. Ambler and Festus P. Summers, *West Virginia: The Mountain State* (Englewood Cliffs, N.J., 1958), chpts. 15-16 & 19 and Richard Orr Curry, *A House Divided: Statehood Politics & the Copperhead Movement in West Virginia* (Pittsburgh, 1964).

    Arthur Ingram Boreman, born in Waynesboro, Pennsylvania, on July 24, 1823, became West Virginia's first governor. When he was four his parents moved to Middlebourne in Tyler County. He studied and read law under his brother, William Boreman. Admitted to the bar in 1845, he moved to Parkersburg on the Ohio River in the following year. There he practiced law and entered politics. He served in the Virginia House of Delegates from 1855-1861. Boreman opposed secession and became active in the statehood movement in western Virginia. He was selected as president of the Second Wheeling Convention (June 11-25, 1861) and served in the reorganized state government. Under the newly reorganized government he served as a circuit judge. With the admission of West Virginia pending, the Constitutional Union party, meeting in Parkersburg, after a four way battle chose him as its gubernatorial candidate. In the general election he was unopposed and chosen the state's first governor. He was reelected in 1864 and 1866. Boreman soon became a member of

100

the Republican party. Resigning from office in 1869, he served in the United States Senate until 1875. At the end of his term he returned to Parkersburg and practiced law and in 1888 was elected to the bench as a circuit judge. He died in 1896. See "Boreman, Arthur Ingram," *Dictionary of American Biography* (New York, 1964), I, pp. 461-462 and John G. Morgan, *West Virginia Governors* (Charleston, W.Va, 1981), pp. 9-15.

George Washington Adams estimates that some 12,000 doctors served in the Union army by the end of the war. Of this number, the largest group— some 2,109 surgeons and 3,882 assistant surgeons—were those appointed by state governors. The examination system employed by the states varied greatly from strict examinations to private ones to none at all. George Washington Adams, *Doctors in Blue: The Medical History of the Union Army in the Civil War* (New York, 1961), pp. 47-48.

2. *History of Delaware County and Ohio* (Chicago: O. L. Baskin & Co., Historical Publishers, 1880), p. 556. *A Centennial Biographical History of the City of Columbus and Franklin County Ohio* (Chicago, 1901), p. 343, reported that John Walker had served as a captain in the Revolutionary War and that Neil's ancestors were from England. *Franklin County at the Beginning of the Twentieth Century* (Columbus, Ohio, 1901) noted that the Walker family was a prominent Virginia family.

   Charles Neil was born in 1807 and died in 1882. Esther Weygandt Powell, comp., *Tombstone Inscriptions and Other Records of Delaware County, Ohio* (Esther Weygandt Powell, 1972), p. 438.

3. The other Neil sons were Charles Wesley (died 1848), James (1833-1868), and John (1835-1909). John Neil also became a doctor. He attended the schools of Delaware County and Ohio Wesleyan University. He received his medical degree from the Starling Medical College in Columbus, Ohio. Powell, *Tombstone Inscriptions*, pp. 67 and 438; Silas W. Fowler, *History of Medicine and Biographical Sketches of the Physicians of Delaware County, Ohio 1804-1910* (Columbus, Ohio, 1910), pp. 76-77.

4. *Thirty-Sixth Announcement of Lectures of the Medical College of Ohio for the Session of 1855-1856* (Cincinnati, 1855), pp. 7-9.

5. Irving A. Watson, *Physicians and Surgeons of America* (Concord, New Hampshire, 1896), p. 704; *Franklin County at the Beginning;* and *Centennial Biographical History of Columbus*, p. 343. The biographical information on Neil is at a considerable variance as to the date of his degree, his entry into military service, and on a trip to London to continue his studies. The above volumes indicate that the degree was granted in 1861 and it is implied that he entered the army thereafter. The *Journal of American Medical Association* (Chicago, 1901), Vol. 36, p. 586, indicates that it was in 1863, and his own letters prove that he entered the army in the summer of 1863. William B. Atkinson, ed., *The Physicians and Surgeons of the United States* (Philadelphia, 1878), p. 306, reported that he had received his M.D. from the Medical College of Ohio in 1860, and immediately thereafter he went to London to continue his studies at St. Bartholomew's and Guy's hospital. Atkinson further indicates that he returned in 1861 and entered the army. This information is interesting for the date of its publication (1878) but does not conform to fact. In the Medical College of Ohio, *Annual Announcement of Lectures for the Session of 1863-4 and Catalogue of Students and Graduates for the Sessions of 1862-3* (Cincinnati, 1863), p. 6, Alexander Neil is listed as having been a student there in the 1862-63 session and A. Longwell as his preceptor. Watson's *Physicians and Surgeons of America* (1896), p. 704, indicates that Neil went to London in 1867 where he spent the year at St. Bartholomew Hospital and Guy's Hospital. If he received his degree in 1861, he probably continued to attend lectures at the Medical College of Ohio as indicated by its *Annual Announcement* until just prior to his

entry into the military, but it is more than probable that he was granted his M.D. in 1863, despite the reiteration of the 1861 date in his Columbus obituary. Columbus *Dispatch*, February 14, 1901.

The Cincinnati College of Medicine and Surgery, founded by Alvan H. Baker who governed the school with a strong personal hand, was chartered in 1851 as the Cincinnati Medical and Surgical College. However, it never granted degrees using that name. Its reputation before 1865 was mixed. It was a rival of the Medical College of Ohio. The college closed in 1902. Goss, *Cincinnati—The Queen City*, II, pp. 244-246; Charles Cist, *Sketches and Statistics of Cincinnati in 1859* (Cincinnati, 1859), pp. 185-186; Otto Juettner, *Daniel Drake and His Followers: Historical and Biographical Sketches* (Cincinnati), pp. 289-294; John B. Shotwell, *A History of the Schools of Cincinnati* (Cincinnati, 1902), pp. 506-508.

The Medical College of Ohio was founded by Daniel Drake, an early pioneer in the founding of a number of medical schools and was chartered by the state legislature in 1819. Along with the Cincinnati College of Medicine and Surgery it was "of the regular Old School in Medicine." In 1857 the Medical College began a process of absorbing the Miami Medical College. Four faculty members of the Miami school were elected to the Ohio school and four more in the following year. The dominating personality at the school in the late 1850s and early 1860s was Dr. George C. Blackman. In a major confrontation involving Blackman the faculty resigned over his actions in 1859. In 1896 the school merged with and became the Medical Department of the University of Cincinnati. Juettner, *Daniel Drake*, pp. 21-211; Otto Juettner, "Rise of Medical Colleges in the Ohio Valley," *Ohio Archaeological and Historical Publications*, vol. 22, pp. 487-489; David A. Tucker, Jr., "Some Early Landmarks in the Medical History of Cincinnati," *The Ohio State Medical Journal*, vol. 18 (Jan., 1942), pp. 55-58; *Centennial Year Book: College of Medicine—University of Cincinnati* (Cincinnati, 1921), pp. 21-24; Cist, *Cincinnati in 1859*, pp. 182-186.

6. The 12th West Virginia Regiment was organized and mustered into United States service on August 30, 1862. It drew its members from Marshall, Ohio, Harrison, Marion, Taylor, Hancock, and Brooke counties of then western Virginia. William Hewitt, *History of the Twelfth West Virginia Infantry* (Published by the Twelfth West Virginia Volunteer Infantry Association), pp. 6-7.
7. Neil to Friends, May 12, 1865, Neil Papers.
8. Neil to People, June 7, 1865, and to Friends, June 12, 1865, ibid.
9. Neil to Dear Friends, June 22, 1865, ibid.
10. Fowler, *Medicine and Biographical Sketches*, p. 76.
11. Neil to Dear Friends, July 21 & 23, 1864, ibid.
12. *Centennial Biographical History of Columbus*, p. 343; *Franklin County at the Beginning*; and Columbus *Dispatch*, February 14, 1901. Neil and his wife had four children. One died in infancy, while three daughters, Gamma, Dessie, and Goldie, survived their father.
13. Watson, *Physicians and Surgeons of America*, p. 704; *A Centennial Biographical History*, p.343.
14. Neil briefly testified that he met Guiteau, probably in 1878, when the defendant attempted to sell him a pamphlet on the "Coming of Christ." Neil recalled that at the time he had indicated to friends that he believed Guiteau "was a lunatic." *Report of the Proceedings in the Case of the United States vs Charles J. Guiteau* (Washington, 1882), I, pp. 714-715; Charles E. Rosenberg, *The Trial of the Assassin Guiteau* (Chicago, 1963), p. 142.
15. Columbus *Dispatch*, February 14, 1901.

CHAPTER I

1. See Alexander Neil to Dear Friends, May 19, 1864, Neil Papers.
2. In the lower Valley two smaller lines, the Manassas Gap and the Winchester and Potomac railroads, lay in shambles from the military operations in the early part of the war. Only the Baltimore and Ohio Railroad, entering the Valley at Harper's Ferry and passing through Martinsburg to the west, remained in active operation in that area. For the Union it was a critical link between the Ohio Valley and Washington and the eastern theatre. The number of Federal troops deployed to guard it attested to its importance. It was a frequent target for guerrillas and Confederate raiders. In protecting the road Harper's Ferry became a major garrison, while Martinsburg functioned as a supply depot for Federal operations in the lower Valley.
3. U. S. War Dept., *The War of the Rebellion: A Compilation of the Official Records of the Union and Confederate Armies* (Washington, 1880-1901), XXXIII, p. 795 [Hereafter cited as *Official Records*]; John Y. Simon, ed., *The Papers of Ulysses S. Grant* (Carbondale, Ill., 1982), vol. 10, pp. 245-246 [Hereafter cited as *Grant Papers*].
4. Simon, *Grant Papers*, vol. 10, pp. 252-253.
   General Halleck, chief of staff, was reported as being "indignant" over Sigel's appointment. Cecil B. Eby, Jr., *A Virginia Yankee in the Civil War* (Chapel Hill, N.C., 1961), p. 214.
5. *Official Records*, XXXIII, p. 1006.
6. *Official Records*, XXXVII, pt. 1, pp. 368-369.
7. Franz Sigel, "Sigel in the Shenandoah Valley in 1864," in *Battles and Leaders of the Civil War* (Repr.: New York, 1956), p. 488.
8. *Official Records*, XXXVII, pt. 1, pp. 467-468; Sigel, "Sigel in the Shenandoah Valley," p. 488. More cautiously Sigel indicated that "If Breckinridge should advance against us I will resist him at some convenient position."
9. Eby, *Virginia Yankee*, p. 224.
10. The mission was badly flawed at the very outset. Moor was not familiar with the Valley. Neither maps nor scouts were supplied to him. Worst of all, his unit was not composed of even his own brigade. Two of Moor's regiments were on escort duty and the two remaining ones were insufficient in themselves for such an assignment. Normally the brigade under Colonel Thoburn should have been used. Later Captain Henry A. Du Pont would charge that Sigel was determined that "the reconnaissance should be commanded by a fellow-German." Even Moor regarded it as "a great mistake." William S. Lincoln, *Life with the Thirty-Fourth Massachusetts Infantry in the War of the Rebellion* (Worcester, Mass., 1879), pp. 281 & 289; Henry A. Du Pont, *The Campaign of 1864 in the Valley of Virginia and Expedition to Lynchburg* (New York, 1925), pp. 9-10; *Official Records*, XXXVII, pt. 1, p. 79; Eby, *Virginia Yankee*, p. 224; William C. Davis, *The Battle of New Market* (Baton Rouge, La., 1975), pp. 70-71.
11. Sigel, "Sigel in the Shenandoah," p. 488; Theodore F. Lang, *Loyal West Virginia from 1861 to 1865* (Baltimore, 1895), p. 113; William H. Beach, *The First New York (Lincoln) Cavalry* (New York, 1902), p. 349.
12. Sigel, "Sigel in the Shenandoah," p. 488; Lang, *Loyal West Virginia*, p. 113; Beach, *First New York Cavalry*, p. 349.
13. *Official Records*, XXXVI, pt. 2, pp. 840-841; Simon, *Grant Papers*, pp. 459-460n.
   An amusing quip by Colonel David Strother quickly made the rounds of the army. "Oh ho! By Jove, boys! The Department of West Virginia is doing a big business. General Averell's tearing up the railroad, and General Sigel's tearing down the 'pike'!" Sigel was not amused. Miles O'Reilly, *Baked Meats* (New York, 1866), pp. 300-301.
14. *Richmond Whig*, June 25, 1864.

15. *Official Records*, XXXVII, pt. 1, pp. 278-279, 480, 500, & 507; pt. 3, pp. 3-4.
16. Eby, *Virginia Yankee*, pp. 231-232.
17. *Official Records*, XXXVII, pt. 1, p. 479.
18. Responding the best that he could, Lee ordered Jones' command to join Imboden. In addition General John C. Vaughn and his Tennessee brigade of cavalry and Colonel William Jackson and his men were ordered to Mount Crawford. Local reserves and government officials in Staunton were also called upon to serve. Jones with the senior commission assumed command of the little army. Milton W. Humphreys noted in his diary that the army "consisted of troops from every quarter, hastily to (?) together, and [some of them] altogether undisciplined." Milton W. Humphreys Diary, June 1-4, p. 83, University of Virginia; Milton W. Humphreys, *A History of the Lynchburg Campaign* (Charlottesville, Va., 1924), pp. 30-31.
19. *Official Records*, XXXVII, pt. 1, p. 543; Simon, *Grant Papers*, vol. 10, pp. 487-488.
20. *Official Records*, XXXVII, pt. 1, pp. 146, 613-614; Martin F. Schmitt, ed., *General George Crook: His Autobiography* (Norman, Okla., 1986), p. 117; Eby, *Virginia Yankee*, pp. 250-251.

    Later, Grant in his personal memoirs, even though he refused "to find fault with him," believed that "Had General Hunter moved by way of Charlottesville, instead of Lexington, as his instructions contemplated, he would have been in a position to have covered the Shenandoah Valley against the enemy, should the force he met have seemed to endanger it." If that force failed to materialize, then as Grant noted, he would have been in striking distance of the James River Canal which would have cut a major line of communication for Lynchburg and which also would have put him between the city and Lee's detachment which was sent to defend it. U. S. Grant, *Personal Memoirs of U. S. Grant* (Repr.: New York), II, p. 574.
21. In a report on the Lynchburg campaign, Colonel David Strother, Hunter's chief of staff, noted a number of reasons for the decision to retreat. Prisoners, captured from Ewell's corps, told them that Grant had suffered a setback at Petersburg, that General Philip Sheridan's attempt to join Hunter's army via Charlottesville had failed, and that Lee had sent a large force under Jubal Early to defend Lynchburg. As Strother indicated, "It was now evident that the Army of West Virginia was in a critical position." Fearing that Early's army was much its superior and noting that the army was some two hundred and fifty miles from its base and that its ammunition was close to exhaustion as well as its commissariat, for Hunter and his staff there was no other decision but retreat. Hunter's greatest fear was that the Confederates would attack before they could successfully withdraw under cover of darkness. David Strother, "Operations in West Virginia: Report of Colonel Strother," in Frank Moore, ed., *The Rebellion Record: A Diary of American Events* (New York), XI, p. 487.
22. General Benjamin Franklin Kelley, born in New Hampshire, moved to Wheeling, Virginia, when he was 19, served almost his entire military service in Maryland and Virginia protecting the Baltimore and Ohio Railroad. At the outbreak of the war he raised the 1st Virginia Regiment and participated in the battle of Philippi. Wounded there, he was commissioned a brigadier general. Ezra J. Warner, *Generals in Blue* (Baton Rouge, La., 1964), pp. 260-261.
23. Major General Franz Sigel, born in Sinsheim, Baden, in 1824, was a graduate of a military academy at Carlsruhe. In the uprisings of 1848 he served as an officer in the German Republican Army in an attempt to overthrow the Grand Duke of Baden. Unfortunately, his service demonstrated more political acumen than military leadership. With the collapse of the revolt he fled to England and then moved to New York in 1852. There, he temporarily taught before moving to St. Louis where he became Director of Schools and taught as a professor of mathematics in the German Institute. Increasingly he assumed a promi-

nent role in the German-American community. At the outbreak of the war he helped to organize the home guards. Initially he demonstrated military promise in helping to secure Missouri for the Union. As a hero of several small engagements and with his obvious political significance, he was made a brigadier general. His defeat at the Battle of Wilson's Creek, however, quickly tarnished that luster. Yet Sigel remained popular with the Germans, and they continued to press for his advancement. What military accomplishments failed to achieve, politics did. In March 1862 he was promoted to major general. His performance, with the exception of the Battle of Pea Ridge in Arkansas, remained poor. Finally, at his own request in February 1863 he was relieved of command for "medical reasons."

However, in early 1864 a configuration of factors secured his appointment as commander of the Department of West Virginia. State legislators petitioned a receptive Lincoln for a change there. Also obvious was the president's taking into account the forthcoming presidential election and the German vote. Colonel David Hunter Strother, better known as "Porte Crayon" and a member of General Kelley's staff, cynically recorded in his diary that "the Dutch vote must be secured at all hazards for the Government and the sacrifice of West Virginia is a small matter." It would also solve another problem, what to do with a shelved major general. Then, there was also Sigel who lobbied for it. "Franz Sigel, U.S.A, 1824-1902," in Walton Rawls, ed., *Great Civil War Heroes and Their Battles* (New York, 1985), pp. 149-151; Davis, *Battle of New Market*, pp. 7-10; Eby, *Virginia Yankee*, pp. 213-214.

24. Petersburg, not to be confused with the town south of Richmond and key to the defense of the Confederate capital, is located on the South Branch of the Potomac River, some twelve miles to the southwest of Moorefield in West Virginia.

25. Major Richard H. Brown; Captain Jacob H. Bristor; First Lieutenant John R. Brenneman; and Second Lieutenant Elam F. Pigott. Lang, *Loyal West Virginia*, pp. 282-284.

26. General Kelley remained in the Department of West Virginia but assigned to supervise the guarding of the railroad from west of Monocacy Junction in Maryland through West Virginia. *Official Records*, XXXVII, pt. 1, pp. 408, 414.

27. Captain William L. Roberts; First Lieutenants Thomas H. Means and Francis H. Pierpont, Jr.

28. Rumors of poor treatment of Federal prisoners in Richmond spurred Federal authorities to attempt a surprise raid to secure their release. Believing that Richmond was defended only by militia and thus vulnerable, Brigadier General Judson Kilpatrick with a force of nearly 3,600 led the expedition on February 28. On the following day Colonel Ulric Dahlgren with 500 men split off from the main group and moved towards Goochland. Kilpatrick reached the Richmond defenses on March 1, but finding the element of surprise gone and the city's defenses formidable, he aborted the attempt. In the meantime Dahlgren, encountering various difficulties and strong resistance, was trapped and killed in his attempt to retreat. Papers on Dahlgren's body "exhorting the prisoners [Federal] to destroy and burn the hateful city and kill the traitor Davis and his cabinet" have caused controversy ever since. *Official Records*, XXXIII, pp. 169-224.

29. Dr. John Neil (1835-1909) was the eldest of the Neil brothers.

30. Lieutenant Colonel Robert S. Northcott.

31. In Lee's move north in June 1863, General Richard Ewell's Second Corps moved through Chester Gap into the Valley and marched on Winchester. Major General Milroy with slightly over 5,000 troops intended initially to stand his ground, then decided to retreat, and was badly routed at Stephenson's Depot. Some 3,358 Federals were captured by Ewell. The 12th West Virginia

lost 3 officers and 41 enlisted men in the battle. After surrendering, they were taken to Richmond and later reactivated. Marshall Brice, *Conquest of a Valley* (University Press of Virginia, 1965), p. 66; Mark M. Boatner III, *The Civil War Dictionary* (New York, 1959), p. 937. See Wilbur Sturtevant Nye, *Here Come The Rebels!* (Baton Rouge, La., 1965), chpts. 7-8.

32. Rev. S. W. Sears, Baltimore Conference, served in Cumberland during 1863-1865.

33. Dr. John W. Riddle, assistant surgeon, 61st Pennsylvania Volunteers.

34. Kelley, then a colonel commanding advance units of General George B. McClellan's army in western Virginia and after retaking Grafton, struck at Colonel G. A. Porterfield's army in an early morning surprise attack and completely routed the Confederates on June 3, 1861. The ensuing Southern panic came to be known as the "Philippi Races." Kelley was seriously wounded and was recommended and promoted to brigadier general. Lang, *Loyal West Virginia*, pp. 320-321; Warren W. Hassler, Jr., *General George B. McClellan: Shield of the Union* (Baton Rouge, La., 1957), pp. 8-10.

35. Originally General Edward O. C. Ord was assigned the troops that were to make up the column striking at the Tennessee and Virginia Railroad. Difficulties quickly arose between Ord and Sigel. With the refusal of Sigel to supply him with required forces and supplies, Ord asked to be relieved of command. "All this ... mortified me and caused the step I took." *Official Records*, XXXII, p. 183 and XXXVII, pt. 1, pp. 526-527; Bernarr Cresap. *Appomattox Commander* (San Diego, 1981), pp. 119-120.

36. McClellan, following the victory at Philippi, moved his army against General Robert Selden Garnett, commander of the Confederate forces in western Virginia. Garnett had taken up positions on Laurel Hill and Rich Mountain. Under McClellan's direction General William S. Rosecrans took Rich Mountain, and in being outflanked and his position at Laurel Hill threatened, Garnett attempted to escape. At Garrick's Ford on the Shivers fork of the Cheat River Garnett was killed in a rearguard action on July 13. Douglas Southall Freeman, *R. E. Lee* (New York, 1934), I, pp. 532-534; Hassler, *McClellan*, pp. 17-18. For the campaign in western Virginia see *Official Records*, II, pp. 194-292.

37. Martinsburg, a small town at the head of the Shenandoah Valley, was the county seat of Berkeley County. In the 1850s it became an increasingly important commercial center on the Baltimore and Ohio Railroad, and during the Civil War it was used as an important supply depot for Union operations in the lower Valley. The military quickly dominated the town's life and economy. As a military objective it was subject to periodic Southern raids and temporary occupations. The town's churches and public buildings were frequently used as hospitals or barracks. See Vernon Aler, *Aler's History of Martinsburg and Berkeley County, West Virginia* (Hagerstown, Md., 1888).

38. Major General Julius Stahel, Brigadier Generals Jeremiah Cutler Sullivan and Max Weber, who was in command at Harper's Ferry.

39. Jane Boswell Moore (1843-1924) faded into obscurity. Apparently she was the daughter of Gibbons Moore and Ann Barrieve. She became the second wife of Frederick Ehlen Gambrill and had one son, Frederick Moore Gambrill. Dielman File, Maryland Historical Society, Baltimore, Maryland.

40. On the original letter Neil, reflecting the change in the P.S., drew a large X over the last two paragraphs.

41. Bunker Hill was a small town halfway between Martinsburg and Winchester.

42. Lieutenant Colonel James Faulkner, a Democrat and a former member of Virginia state legislature and Congressman from Martinsburg, was appointed Ambassador to France in 1859 by President James Buchanan. On his return to the United States in 1861 he was arrested by Union authorities. After his release he joined the Confederacy and served on General Thomas "Stonewall" Jackson's

staff as his chief of staff. Faulkner wrote the drafts for Jackson's battle reports. His two sons also served in the Confederate army. In 1864 General David Hunter ordered Faulkner's home burned, but on appeal to Lincoln by his wife the president intervened and prevented the order from being carried out. Aler, *Aler's History of Martinsburg*, pp. 314-334; J. E. Norris, ed., *History of the Lower Shenandoah Valley* (Chicago, 1890), pp. 260-261; Lenoir Chambers, *Stonewall Jackson* (New York, 1959), II, pp. 313-314.

Neil came in contact with Mrs. Faulkner in August, 1863. His regiment camped on her estate. He was intrigued by her. On August 5 he wrote, "His lady occupies the fine mansion and as she pretends to be Union we have placed a guard around her house and over her flower beds, and *woe* to the man who dares to molest a flower," and on the following day "I advised the guards to be sure and observe the *rights of property*," but he noted, "still whilst they took their turns in watching the garden, to avail themselves of a mess of potatoes & peas occasionally, and say nothing about it." Neil to Dear Friends, August 5-6, 1863, Neil Papers.

In a letter to the Wheeling *Daily Intelligencer*, dated August 12, he wrote: "Mrs. F. and her daughter, a beautiful girl of some eighteen summers, are the only occupants of the house, and have been staunch Union women from the beginning. They are very kind to our soldiers, especially the sick, and contribute many nice things for their comfort as well as furnish a great deal of reading matter from the Colonel's library for the boys to peruse." Wheeling, W.Va., *Daily Intelligencer*, August 14, 1863.

Later, he could write home that "I have called several times on Mrs. Faulkner and her daughter, at their princely mansion and have been treated like a gentleman." He further noted that "Mrs. F. is very kind to our soldiers, giving them, especially the sick, many nice things to eat and furnishing plenty of reading matter for the boys." Neil to Dear Friends at Home, August 16, 1863, Neil Papers.

Ten days later in the *Daily Intelligencer* "Veritas" took Neil to task "for I can not believe that any member of our regiment would have so far forgotten himself, as to write, and send for publication, such a medley of high sounding phrases and absurdities, couched in words of such 'learned length and thundering sound'." The writer poked fun at his "fertile imagination." "Veritas" concluded that "when this was written, we must conclude that the young ladies of Martinsburg have very susceptible hearts, or that the author has formed a very erroneous opinion concerning them." *Daily Intelligencer*, August 24, 1863.

However, Theodore F. Lang, writing in 1895 in his *Loyal West Virginia*, verifies Neil's view. He noted that Mrs. Faulkner and her daughters entertained General Averell and his staff several times "at the pleasant and hospitable mansion" and "their native hospitality gave a welcome to either Union or Confederate gentlemen, whether in or out of the army." Lang, *Loyal West Virginia*, p.118.

43. Winchester was a town of 4,403 people on the eve of the Civil War. It was the commercial center and county seat of Frederick County. The town was a hub for roads running north and south and east and west. It was also linked to the Main Line of the Baltimore and Ohio Railroad at Harper's Ferry by the Winchester & Potomac Railroad; technologically it was a poor and antiquated railroad. In the first year of the war military operations destroyed the rail line's use. On the eve of the war Unionist sentiment dominated the area, but with Virginia's secession public sentiment in Winchester and Frederick County radically changed in support of the Confederacy. Strategically located in the lower Valley it was a focal point from which Southern armies could threaten the Baltimore and Ohio Railroad and strike into Maryland and Pennsylvania. For a Federal army occupying the town there were definite advantages. It not only safeguarded the railroad and Maryland but protected Washington's right flank as well. A Union army there also posed a potential threat to Staunton and the

Virginia Central Railroad some 100 miles to the south in the upper Valley. Winchester frequently changed hands during the Civil War. See Frederic Morton, *The Story of Winchester in Virginia* (Strasburg, Va., 1925), chpts. 7-9; Jeffrey N. Lash, *Destroyer of the Iron Horse: General Joseph E. Johnston and Confederate Rail Transport, 1861-1865* (Kent, Ohio, 1991), pp. 9-12.

44. First Families of Virginia.
45. On the day of Sigel's entry into Winchester Colonel John Mosby's men struck a wagon train near Bunker Hill capturing eight wagons. Then that night he stealthily entered Martinsburg, Sigel's base, and captured and carried off several prisoners and fifteen horses. Much to the embarrassment of the Federal garrison the exploit was not known until morning. Charles Wells Russell, ed., *Memoirs of Colonel John S. Mosby* (Bloomington, Ind., 1959), pp. 272-273.
46. Richard W. Wallace.
47. Grant and Lee had just finished the battle of the Wilderness, the first of a series of battles on the road to Richmond. On May 7 Grant began his push towards Spotsylvania Court House.
48. Captain John McNeill and his partisan rangers directed a raid against Piedmont, West Virginia, in early May. Piedmont was a railroad center which contained seven shops and other railroad equipment. With sixty rangers McNeill struck first at Bloomington and then at Piedmont. Within an hour they had destroyed more than a million dollars worth of property. To add insult to injury, McNeill sent six locomotive engines at full steam down the rail line towards New Creek. Roger U. Delauter, Jr., *McNeill's Rangers* (Lynchburg, Va., 1986), pp. 66-67; Robert White, "West Virginia," *Confederate Military History* (Repr., Blue and Grey Press), p. 121; Simeon Miller Bright, "The McNeill Rangers: A Study in Confederate Guerilla Warfare," *West Virginia History*, pp. 353-356; *Official Records*, XXXVII, pt. 1, p. 69.
49. Grant and Lee clashed on May 10 at Spotsylvania. Union forces were repulsed in their assaults on Confederate lines.
50. For an excellent account of the Battle of New Market see Davis, *Battle of New Market*.
51. Brigadier General John Daniel Imboden was appointed to command the Valley District on July 28, 1863. A native of Augusta County, Virginia, he organized the Staunton Artillery, a light battery, and was elected its captain in 1859. In May of 1861 he and his battery left for Harper's Ferry to secure that point. He participated and performed well in the first battle of Bull Run and received the praise of "Stonewall" Jackson as a "dauntless leader." In the spring of 1862 he organized a group of partisan rangers to conduct raids on the Baltimore and Ohio Railroad, but later in that year the War Department, wanting to reduce the number of independent organizations operating in western Virginia, transferred him and his men to regular service. His cavalry participated in the Gettysburg campaign and operated on General Richard Ewell's left flank. Unfortunately, a blunder in the campaign would mar his record. When Lee needed his services, he was resting at Hancock, Maryland, some 50 miles southwest of Gettysburg. Lee was furious. Imboden partially redeemed himself in the retreat by holding off a Federal attack on Lee's wagon train until Stuart could arrive with additional support. Later, Imboden and General Jubal Early clashed. Early charged that his command was "in a very bad state of discipline." Despite reservations, Imboden remained in command of the Valley District. In the spring of 1864 Imboden had only a little over 2,000 men spread over a large area. *Official Records*, XXXIII, pp. 1167-1168; Douglas Southall Freeman, *Lee's Lieutenants* (New York, 1946), III, p. 48; Davis, *New Market*, pp. 18-19; Haviland Harris Abbot, "General John D. Imboden," *West Virginia History* (Jan. 1960), XXI, pp. 88-111.

52. Reference to Longstreet was an error. Longstreet was with Lee on May 6. He helped to fend off a Federal assault and was seriously wounded. He would not return to Lee's service until October. Freeman, *Lee's Lieutenants*, II, pp. 356–368, 613.
53. Twenty-two pieces.
54. More accurately 93.
55. Rain and the swollen Smith Creek and the Shenandoah River probably saved much of the Federal army from capture. Breckinridge had conceived a brilliant plan of sending Imboden with the 18th Virginia Cavalry down the east side of Smith Creek to recross it near its mouth and then to strike at the bridge and destroy it before the Union army could cross the river to safety. If the plan had been executed, Sigel's army would have been trapped. However, high water, and Imboden's feeble attempt to cross the stream left the Federals' route of escape open. Davis, *New Market*, p. 150; Roger U. Delauter, Jr., *The 18th Virginia Cavalry* (Lynchburg, Va., 1985), p. 21.
56. Colonel George Wells.
57. The 12th West Virginia's performance at New Market was mixed at best. Placed in the rear of the 34th Massachusetts Regiment, they were unable to fire for fear of hitting the Massachusetts' men. But they also failed to take advantage of a gap in Wharton's Confederate line, and they failed to support Carlin's battery which had come under severe fire. Worst of all the West Virginians attached themselves to Sigel, and as he attempted to reconnoiter the field, they followed him. That forced the general to remain between his batteries and the Massachusetts' men. In Sigel's counter-charge, the West Virginians remained in reserve. The men who had gone to the support of the batteries performed no better. Despite orders to advance against the Confederates to give Carlin and Snow's batteries time to retreat, they failed to obey. Davis, *New Market*, pp. 130–133 & 141.

   The West Virginians were sensitive to the criticism of their role in the battle. They maintained that they were placed in a position where as William Hewitt later wrote, "we could not fire on the enemy without firing into our own men, and yet so close to the front line that we suffered severely from the enemies fire." Hewitt, *History of the Twelfth West Virginia*, p. 110.
58. Lieutenant Colonel William S. Lincoln.
59. Major General David Hunter, a radical abolitionist, martinet, arbitrary and independent minded, assumed command of the Department of West Virginia on May 21. Hunter was born in Washington, D.C. in 1802 and had family connections in northern Virginia, especially the Shenandoah Valley. He was the son of Andrew Hunter, a Presbyterian chaplain, and Mary Stockton, the sister of Richard Stockton, a signer of the Declaration of Independence. Hunter was a graduate of West Point. After graduation he served on the western frontier and was promoted to captain in 1833. Feisty in his early career, he was convicted by court-martial of insubordination, but the sentence was remitted, probably in deference to family connections, by President John Quincy Adams. He resigned his commission in 1836 to become a real estate speculator in Chicago. However, he resumed his military career in 1841 in the paymaster office of the army. He served in a noncombatant role in the Mexican War and on the eve of the Civil War he was serving in Kansas.

   Hunter's predilection to politics forged a number of very important contacts for him. He informed Lincoln of various presumed plots to prevent him from being inaugurated. He accompanied the president on his trip to Washington. Additional contacts brought him favor. He was promoted to colonel of the 6th United States Cavalry, and a month later he was placed in charge of the right division of General Irwin McDowell's army. In the battle of First Manassas he suffered a severe neck wound and escaped any blame for the Union defeat.

Instead, he was appointed a brigadier general of Volunteers and then a major general. In a meteoric rise he was in September 1861 the fourth ranking major general in the Volunteers.

After recovering he was assigned to the Western Department. In the controversy over the handling of that department by General John C. Fremont he testified on affairs in Missouri before the Committee on the Conduct of the War. In the sometimes rough and hostile interrogatory by the committee, Hunter, who was both politically sensitive and militarily ambitious, quickly realized the importance of currying favor with the radicals. Hunter succeeded Fremont briefly; then was reassigned to the Department of Kansas. Using political connections, he secured a transfer to the Department of the South. There he became involved in controversy over his issuing of an emancipation proclamation in May 1862. The edict was revoked by Lincoln. Late in 1863 Secretary of War Edwin B. Stanton sent him on an inspection trip to report on Grant, then at Chattanooga. Then he was sent to inspect General Nathaniel Banks' command on the Red River. The War Department offered him a command on the West coast, but he preferred a position under Grant instead. Sigel's defeat at New Market opened up that possibility, and Hunter became the commander of the Department of West Virginia. See David Hunter, *Report of the Military Services of Gen. David Hunter, U.S.A.* (New York, 1873); Robert C. Schenck, "Major-General David Hunter," *Magazine of American History* (New York, 1887), XVII; T. Harry Williams, *Lincoln and the Radicals* (New York, 1952); and Edward G. Longacre, "A Profile of Major General David Hunter," *Civil War Times Illustrated* (Jan., 1978), XVI.

The authorities in Washington were horrified by Sigel's defeat. Halleck wired Grant that "Instead of advancing on Staunton he is already in full retreat on Strasburg. If you expect anything from him you will be mistaken. He will do nothing but run. He never did anything else." Stanton proposed Hunter as Sigel's replacement. Grant was told that he would be appointed, "if you desire it." Grant's reply was quick, "By all means I would say appoint Genl. Hunter or any one else to the command of West Virginia." *Official Records*, XXXVI, pt. 2, pp. 840–841 and XXXVII, pt.1, pp. 485 & 492; Simon, *Grant Papers*, vol. 10, pp. 459–460n.

Hunter was well aware of the sensitive political nature of Sigel's removal. Sigel was also aware of the damage of the defeat to him. To repair some of the damage he indicated to Hunter that "actuated by an earnest patriotism, was anxious to take a division in the army or attend to any other duty." Hunter felt that it would be best to place him in command of the forces protecting the Baltimore & Ohio Railroad. Accordingly, Sigel was assigned to command the reserves at Martinsburg and those defending the railroad. Major General David Hunter to Secretary of War Edwin B. Stanton, May 22, 1864, #5, folder 1, Franz Sigel Papers, Western Reserve Historical Society, Cleveland, Ohio: *Official Records*, XXXVII, pt. 1, pp. 507–508, 517.

60. In General Orders No. 29 Hunter underscored the necessity of making the army efficient and called upon it to make sacrifices and suffer to achieve complete success. He directed that "For the expedition on hand, the clothes each soldier has on his back, with one pair of extra shoes and socks, are amply sufficient. . . ." Since the army would be subsisting off of the countryside, "Cattle, sheep, and hogs, and if necessary horses and mules, must be taken and slaughtered." *Official Records*, XXXVII, pt. 1, pp. 517–518.

Corporal William M. Goudy of Company G, 1st West Virginia Volunteer Infantry, recorded in his diary that they "received our knapsacks[,] packed & sent our extra clothing to Martinsburg[,] drew 4 days rations of crackers." To the men of the 116th Ohio Regiment, "This order looked like 'business.'" For William S. Lincoln of the 34th Massachusetts Regiment, "The iron hand of the new

Commander is already felt." Diary of William M. Goudy, May 24, 1864, Civil War
Diaries Collection, West Virginia University; Thos. F. Wildes, *Record of the One
Hundred and Sixteenth Regiment Ohio Infantry Volunteers* (Sandusky, Ohio, 1884),
p. 90; Lincoln, *Thirty-Fourth Massachusetts Infantry*, p. 292.

61. Initially Hunter was cautious about a move up the Valley towards Staunton.
Breckinridge's presence was an inhibiting factor. In his diary Colonel David
Strother, his chief-of-staff, wrote, "It looks therefore as if we could do no more
than demonstrations. We cannot go safely beyond Mt. Jackson . . ." However,
Breckinridge's return to Lee's army radically changed the situation in the Valley. By May 24 Grant reported to Halleck that Breckinridge was "unquestion-
ably here." He indicated to Halleck that "if Hunter can possibly get to
Charlottesville and Lynchburg, he should do so, living on the country." Halleck
in relaying Grant's instructions to Hunter closed with the charge, "In your movements live as much as possible on the country." Eby, *Virginia Yankee*, pp. 231–
232; *Official Records*, XXXVI, pt. 1, pp. 7–8 and pt. 3, pp. 208–209, XXXVII, pt. 1,
pp. 535–536 & 543.

62. The battle of North Anna ended on May 26. Grant's army still retained the
offensive and moved to Lee's right towards Hanovertown.

63. Staunton was the county seat of Augusta County. On the eve of the Civil War it
was Unionist in sentiment and voted overwhelmingly for John Bell on the Con-
stitutional Union ticket. Its citizens opposed the calling of a state convention,
but with the secession of Virginia and the call for arms political sentiment
shifted in support of the Confederacy. Staunton with a population of 3,875
was a very important commercial and agricultural center in the upper
Shenandoah Valley. It had three banks and hotels and some eighty business
houses. The town was also a transportation hub. Roads, including the important macadamized Valley Pike, crossed east and west and north and south
there. It was also directly linked to Charlottesville and Richmond by the Virginia Central Railroad. During the war it became an important military depot,
hospital center, and remount and training point. Until June 1864 Staunton had
defied capture by Federal forces. Jos. A. Waddell, *Annals of Augusta County,
Virginia* (Repr.: Harrisonburg, Virginia, 1979); J. Lewis Peyton, *History of Augusta County, Virginia* (Bridgewater, Virginia, 1953); Richard K. Mac Master,
Augusta County History 1865-1950 (Staunton, Virginia, 1987); and Marshall
Moore Brice, *Conquest of a Valley* (Verona, Va., 1963).

64. For a excellent account of the Battle of Piedmont see Brice, *Conquest of a Valley*.

65. With the return of General Breckinridge to Lee's army Brigadier General William
Edmondson "Grumble" Jones was temporarily placed in command of the Department of Southwestern Virginia and was directed by Lee to defend the Valley against Hunter. *Official Records*, pt. 1, pp. 748, 750-751.

Jones initially concentrated his small force on the south bank of the North
River. As Milton W. Humphreys noted, they "consisted of troops from every
quarter, hastily to [?] together, and [some of them] altogether undisciplined."
Well positioned and confident Jones awaited the Federals. Hunter, however,
had no wish to attack the Confederates at such a formidable site. Instead, as
his army moved out of Harrisonburg, he sent a cavalry force under Lieutenant
Meigs towards Mt. Crawford as a feint. The main army turned left onto the Port
Republic road leading to that town. The movement caught Jones by surprise,
but he quickly moved to counter Hunter's flanking movement. Milton W.
Humphreys Diary, June 1-4, 1864; Brice, *Conquest of a Valley*, pp. 29-30; "Hunter's
Raid, 1864," *Southern Historical Society Papers*, vol. 36, pp. 99-100; Imboden,
"Battle of Piedmont," p. 460; Imboden, "Fire, Sword, and Halter," p. 173;
Humphreys, *History of Lynchburg Campaign*, p. 31.

66. Estimates vary as to Confederate casualties. Marshall M. Brice in *Conquest of Valley* places the figure generally at 1,500 dead, wounded and captured. For officers, he indicates that it is impossible to determine. Federal losses were higher than Hunter, who was prone to minimize, estimated in his official report. He estimated 500, which for accuracy probably should have been closer to 900. Brice indicates that "Based upon various summaries, a liberal estimate might be 150 dead, 650 wounded, and 75 missing."
    The large number of Confederate prisoners in the field posed a serious problem for the Federals. They were merely disarmed and told to give themselves up to any cavalryman in the rear. Brice, *Conquest of Valley*, pp. 77-79.
67. The 12th West Virginia were not a part of the critical turning movement which broke the Confederate line. Their position was on the original line. Brice, *Conquest of Valley*, p. 68.
68. Inverted green chevrons were used by the ambulance detail to designate their rank. Adams, *Doctors in Blue*, pp. 84-85.
    Hospital stewards also wore sashes. The *Hospital Steward's Manual*, written in 1863, specified: "Sash, 'redworsted' sash, with worsted bullion fringe ends; to go twice around the waist, and to tie behind the left hip, pendant part not to be extended more than 18 inches below the tie." Quoted in Gordon Dammann, *Pictorial Encyclopedia of Civil War Medical Instruments and Equipment* (Missoula, Montana, 1983), p. 76.
69. General Crook's movement against the Virginia and Tennessee Railroad and the New River bridge was successful. The depot at Dublin was destroyed and extensive damage to track and the bridge over the New River was inflicted on the railroad. Averell's attempt to strike at Wytheville and Saltville was repulsed by the Confederates. Averell's cavalry moved rapidly to join Crook's column in withdrawing back into West Virginia. On assuming command Hunter quickly reiterated Sigel's order to Crook to move on Staunton. *Official Records*, XXXVII, pt. 1, pp. 278-279 & 480.
70. Lexington with a population of 1,544 free persons was the county seat of agriculturally rich Rockbridge County. It was the region's commercial center. It was not, however, a military depot of warehouses nor was it a transportation hub, although a branch of the James River Canal along the North River connected Lexington to the main line of the canal and with Lynchburg. Along with the array of saddlers, coachmakers, lawyers, and a sundry of other occupations it was the site of the Virginia Military Institute, Washington College (later to become Washington and Lee University), and the home of John Letcher, former governor of the state at secession. When Colonel William S. Lincoln of the 34th Massachusetts Regiment saw the county's wheat fields, he was so impressed that he believed they "would seem to be enough to supply the wants of Lee's entire army. Lovely indeed, almost beyond conception of those who have never seen it, is this whole region." Edwin L. Dooley, Jr., "Lexington in the 1860 Census," *Proceedings of the Rockbridge Historical Society* (Lexington, Va., 1982), IX, pp. 189-196; Lincoln, *Thirty-Fourth Massachusetts Infantry*, p. 307.
71. Brigadier General John McCausland, engaging in delaying tactics, briefly skirmished with Crook's advanced units before the town. He burnt the bridge over North River and deployed a thin line of skirmishers, including the cadets of V.M.I., along the heights of the river. The skirmishing lasted only a few hours, sufficient, however, for McCausland's forces to make a safe exit from the town. The corps of cadets was the first to leave and headed for Balcony Falls. After a short bombardment and flanking movements from the West by Crook's infantry and South by Averell's cavalry the remainder of McCausland's small army retreated towards Buchanan. Soon Hunter's troops marched up Main Street, while others swarmed over the town. John Sergeant Wise, *The End of an Era* (New York, 1899), pp. 312-313; William Couper, *One Hundred Years at V.M.I.*

(Richmond, 1959), III, pp. 23–25; Charles W. Turner, ed., "General David Hunter's Sack of Lexington, Virginia, June 1-15, 1864: An Account by Rose Page Pendleton," *Virginia Magazine of History and Biography* (April, 1975), vol. 83, p. 176.

72. Hunter threatened to burn General Francis Henry Smith's house, but since his daughter, Frances Henderson Morrison, was ill, it was spared. Smith was the superintendent of the Virginia Military Institute. Turner, "Hunter's Sack of Lexington," p. 178 & fn. 20; Eby, *Virginia Yankee*, p. 257.

Opinion among Hunter's officers varied over the destruction. Miles Halpine, an aide to Hunter, watched "with feelings of inexpressible regret though fully satisfied of the justice of the act." Many differed. While many felt that in the destruction of the barracks the general was fully justified "by the laws of war," but others agreed with Captain Henry Du Pont who believed that the destruction of the remaining educational buildings "was entirely unnecessary, besides being contrary to the conventions of civilized warfare." General Crook disagreed with the burning of the Institute and the home of former Governor Letcher. Later in his autobiography, reflecting on the act, he wrote, "I did all in my power to dissuade him, but all to no purpose." Colonel Rutherford B. Hayes fully agreed. "This does not suit many of us . . . It is surely bad." Later in a letter to his wife on July 2 he reiterated the sentiment, "And I am glad to say that General Crook's division officers and men were all disgusted with it." O'Reilly, *Baked Meats*, p. 312; Henry A. DuPont, *The Campaign of 1864 in the Valley of Virginia and Expedition to Lynchburg* (New York, 1925), p. 69; Schmitt, *General Crook*, p. 117; Charles Richard Williams, ed., *Diary and Letters of Rutherford B. Hayes* (Columbus, 1922), IV, pp. 473 & 479.

73. Brigadier General George Crook, born in 1828 near Dayton, Ohio, was an 1852 graduate of West Point. Before the Civil War he served in California. In September of 1861 he was appointed colonel of the 36th Ohio Volunteer Infantry. He served in western Virginia. In August 1862 he was promoted to brigadier general, participated in the Maryland campaign of that summer and commanded a brigade in the Battle of South Mountain and Antietam. Returning to western Virginia, he was concerned with the attempt to rid that section of guerrillas and "bushwhackers." In the summer of 1863 he commanded a cavalry division in the Army of the Cumberland. Later in February 1864 he was reassigned to the Department of West Virginia. As commander of the Army of the Kanawha he led the western pincher movement of Grant's plan to strike at the Tennessee and Virginia Railroad. At the Battle of Cloyd's Mountain he defeated southern forces under Brigadier General Albert G. Jenkins. Moving to Dublin, Virginia, he inflicted serious damage on the railroad and the bridge over the New River before retreating back to Meadow Bluff in West Virginia. Warner, *Generals in Blue*, pp. 102–103; Lang, *Loyal West Virginia*, pp. 327–329.

74. Brigadier General William Woods Averell was born in Steuben County, New York, in 1832. He entered West Point in 1851, and after graduating he served in the West. After receiving additional training as a student-officer at the Cavalry School for Practice at Carlisle, Pennsylvania, he returned to duty in the West. At the outbreak of the war, he was on extended leave from the army for wounds suffered from a severe leg wound in an Indian campaign. Returning to duty, Averell was sent to Fort Arbuckle, some 300 miles west of the Arkansas, to order Colonel William H. Emory to move his men to Fort Leavenworth. In the summer of 1861 he was assigned to the staff of General David Porter as an assistant adjutant general. Following the Battle of Bull Run he was temporarily reassigned to Washington on provost duty. In August 1861 he was appointed colonel of the Third Pennsylvania Cavalry, United States Volunteers and commanded a brigade of cavalry defending the capital. With McClellan's army he participated in the Peninsula campaign and was promoted to brigadier general.

In the summer of 1863 he was in command of a cavalry division in northern Virginia. At the engagement at Kelley's Ford he cautiously fended off General Fitzhugh Lee's cavalry but missed the chance to rout him. His performance in the Chancellorsville campaign angered General Joseph Hooker, and he was removed from command. Assigned to organize a force in the Middle Department, he commanded the 4th Separate Brigade in West Virginia. He was charged with driving out Southern forces in the state, and he conducted three expeditions in late 1863. In March 1864 he assumed command of half of Sigel's cavalry. Edward K. Eckert and Nicholas J. Amato, ed., *Ten Years in the Saddle: The Memoir of William Woods Averell* (San Francisco, 1978), pp. 385-404; Edward K. Eckert and Nicholas J. Amato, ed., "'A Long and Perilous Ride,': The Memoirs of William W. Averell." *Civil War Times Illustrated*, XVI (Oct., 1977), pp. 22-30.

75.   Estimates for the battle are difficult but more accurate figures for those engaged can be found in Davis, *Battle of New Market*, appendix A, pp. 193-201.

76.   "Stonewall" Jackson's grave commanded great respect from Union soldiers. On one occasion as an act of singular respect a number of Union officers, including a cavalry general, "pulled some dark roses of the South and strewed them on Jackson's grave, taking away in return—reverently and with uncovered heads—some few blades of clover." The grave was a favorite place to visit. As Hastings Russell noted, the wooden markers were "nearly cut away by our boys, each wishing a sliver as a memento of this gallant officer." The men of the 18th Connecticut made "rings and other trinkets" from the wood. O'Reilly, *Baked Meat*, pp. 314-316; Walker, *Eighteenth Regiment Connecticut*, pp. 249-250; Autobiography of Hastings, June 11, 1864, Russell Hastings Papers, Rutherford B. Hayes Library, Fremont, Ohio: John Booth Diary, June 11, 1864, John Booth Papers, Ohio Historical Society, Columbus, Ohio.

77.   By the time the army had reached Lexington, rations were becoming a problem. Fortunately, a wagon train caught up with the army there, for as Corporal Charles H. Lynch of the 18th Connecticut noted, "Our rations at this time were very low." Charles H. Lynch, *The Civil War Diary* (Privately printed, 1915), pp. 74-75.

     The rationale of sustaining the army off the countryside was badly flawed. Quite correctly the matter of supply lines was a serious problem. Bushwhackers and guerrillas constituted a constant threat. However, periodic shortages of rations had already surfaced during its move to Lexington. Foraging had not been fully satisfactory and the efficiency of the quartermaster was often times in question. William Patterson in Lexington confided to his diary, "Our commissary how incompetent." By the time the 34th Massachusetts reached Buchanan, their hard tack was gone and flour was scarce, although as Colonel Lincoln noted, "We still have beef and mutton in plenty." William Patterson Diary, Southern Historical Collection, University of North Carolina; Lincoln, *Thirty-Fourth Massachusetts*, p. 308.

78.   Corporal James F. Ellis of the 15th West Virginia noted, "The deeds of pillaging, cruelty and robbing done by this army can't be described only by those unfortunate families that this army has passed." Diary of James F. Ellis, June 13, 1864, Roy Bird Cook Collection, West Virginia University.

79.   Several weeks later a group of prisoners from Hunter's army, being taken to Lynchburg on their way to Andersonville, stopped in Lexington overnight. Briefly incarcerated above a storehouse, a mob gathered outside the building and threatened the soldiers with violence and hanging. Finally local military authorities intervened, and the soldiers were taken to the county jail and placed in a secure cell. Frank S. Reader, *History of the Fifth West Virginia Cavalry* (New Brighton, Pa., 1890), p. 284.

80.   Lynchburg with a population of 6,853, located 110 miles west of the Confederate capital on the James River, was the principal commercial center in central Virginia. It was served by a number of transportation lines. Six turnpikes, the

James River and Kanawha Canal, and three railroads—the Virginia and Tennessee Railroad, the Orange and Alexandria Railroad, and the Southside Railroad—linked the city to Richmond, Petersburg and other communities in Virginia. Lynchburg had become a major tobacco center, but the town could also boast a number of industries as well. Four foundries—located in the vicinity tapped the iron ore to the west—a number of grist mills, a clothing manufacturer, a furniture maker, and commission houses also operated there. In addition the city had four banks. On the eve of the Civil War Lynchburg was at the height of its prosperity. Philip Lightfoot Scruggs, *The History of Lynchburg Virginia 1786-1946* (Lynchburg, Va.), p. 96; George S. Morris and Susan L. Foutz, *Lynchburg in the Civil War* (Lynchburg, Va., 1984), chpt. 1; George Graham Morris, "Confederate Lynchburg, 1861-1865" (M.A. thesis, Virginia Polytechnic Institute and State University, 1977), chpt. 1.

The strategic location of Lynchburg for Lee was critical. As a depot with large commissary and quartermaster stores, medical supplies, plus hospitals, and as a transportation hub, its loss would have been devastating for the Army of Northern Virginia. As a rail center it allowed the Confederates considerable flexibility in shifting troops as well as tapping a large area for supplies. Charles M. Blackford, *The Campaign and Battle of Lynchburg* (Lynchburg, 1907), p. 5.

81. On June 12 Lee ordered the detachment of the Second Corps under General Jubal Early to go to check Hunter's moves in the Shenandoah Valley. His initial orders were for him to move into the Valley and strike Hunter's rear and then to advance down the Shenandoah and, if possible, cross the Potomac River to threaten Washington. However, with Lynchburg poorly defended and obviously the intended objective of Hunter, Early quickly moved his army by rail from Charlottesville to Lynchburg. In the meantime units of McCausland and Imboden delayed Hunter's advance which gave Early precious time. At Lynchburg Early, still lacking the full strength of his corps, succeeded in bluffing Hunter. As the Federals reached the outskirts of Lynchburg, Early by using a railroad engine and a few cars along with units of McCausland and Gabe Wharton marching and counter marching, created the illusion of massive enforcement pouring into the city. Hunter, in turn, decided to retreat. Jubal Early, *A Memoir of The Last Year of the War for Independence* (Lynchburg, 1867), pp. 40-41; Frank Vandiver, *Jubal's Raid: General Early's Famous Attack on Washington in 1864* (New York, 1960), chpt. 2.

Hunter in a message from Gauley Bridge to Grant on June 28 cited his reasons for the retreat: "Running short of ammunition, and finding it impossible to collect supplies while in presence of an enemy believed to be superior to our force in numbers and constantly receiving re-enforcement from Richmond and other points, I deemed it best to withdraw. . . ." He also added that it was done "without serious loss." *Official Records*, XXXVII, pt. 1, pp. 683-684.

82. Some 150 wounded were left in a temporary hospital by necessity. Dr. Hayes was given insufficient notice of the intended retreat. Eby, *Virginia Yankee*, pp. 266-267.

83. John T. Booth of the 36th Ohio, noting in his diary on the march to Gauley Bridge, wrote, "Awful Times. No grub to eat. Nearly one third of our command have fallen out by the road side from sheer hunger and exhaustion. We get nothing till we get to Gauley Bridge 47 miles yet." Russell Hastings, an aide to Colonel Rutherford B. Hayes, noted on June 27, "For nine days and nights we marched on making 164 miles with only two days rations with the exception of a small flour and beef issue on the 22nd. Only the provident who husbanded the small supply in their haversack when we left Lynchburg came through with the flag and column. The balance were scattered, some not coming in for several days." Booth Diary, June 26, 1864, Booth Papers; Russell Hastings Diary, June 27, 1864, p. 19, Hastings Papers.

For a perspective from Hunter's staff see Eby, *Virginia Yankee*, pp. 267–275. Colonel David Strother, Hunter's chief of staff, gloomily noted on June 22, "Worn out with fatigue, without supplies in a country producing little at best and already wasted by war, the troops are beginning to show symptoms of demoralization. . . ." Later, Miles Halpine in 1866 described the retreat as "the arduous withdrawal of our nearly starving and ammunitionless forces across the sterile tract of the Catawba and other mountain ranges of the Alleghenies. . . ." Even Hunter acknowledged that the army was in poor shape. In an official report, dated August 8, 1864, Hunter indicated that after arriving at Charleston "their recent fatigues neither men nor animals were in any condition for a farther march, and the excessive heat of the weather would have rendered such an attempt ruinous to the army." Eby, *Virginia Yankee*, p. 269; Miles O'Reilly, *Baked Meats of the Funeral* (New York, 1866), p. 326; *Official Records*, XXXVII, pt. 1, pp. 96–103.

> The men of Sullivan's First Division sang:
> "General Hunter, on the Lynchburg raid,
> D-d near starved the First Brigade,
> Stuval, Stuval, etc."

Wildes, *One Hundred and Sixteenth Regiment*, p. 123.

84. Averell believed that "Its greatness as a military achievement will be recognized by history." Later in a report, requested by Hunter, David Strother summed up the official position, "I have always considered the movement on Lynchburg as one of the boldest and best-conducted campaigns of the war; that the motives which dictated it fully justified the hazard incurred, and that the results obtained by very inadequate forces have been fully acknowledged by those who best understood their real value." Later in July in defense of Hunter for some of the subsequent actions in West Virginia, Grant wrote to C. A. Dana, assistant secretary of war, "He is known to have advanced into the enemy's country, towards their Main Army, inflicting a much greater damage upon them than they have inflicted upon us, with double his force, and moving directly away from our Main Army. . . . I fail to see yet that Gen. Hunter has not acted with great promptness and great success." Later in his autobiography Grant, in continuing to refuse to criticize the campaign, wrote, "The promptitude of his movements and his gallantry should entitle him to the commendation of his country." Eby, *Virginia Yankee*, p. 275; "Report of Colonel Strother, Operations in West Virginia," in Moore, *Rebellion Record*, XI, p. 490; Hunter, *Report of Military Services*, p. 50. Simon, *Grant Papers*, vol. 11, p. 251; Grant, *Personal Memoirs*, II, p. 574.

85. On the retreat from Lynchburg Captain Henry Du Pont, commander of the artillery, witnessed one such case where Hunter became so frustrated by a teamster who was blocking the road that "Snatching the whip from the hand of the astounded wagoner, our commanding general soundly castigated the offender with the instrument with which the latter was wont to belabor his own beasts!" Du Pont, *Campaign of 1864*, p. 87.

86. James R. Hubbell, from Delaware and Republican nominee for the House of Representatives from the Ohio 8th Congressional district, won in the October election over his Democratic opponent, William Johnston. Ben: Perley Poore, *The Political Register and Congressional Directory* (Boston, 1878), pp. 171 and 458.

CHAPTER II

1. Early intentionally took the long route to reach Charlottesville. He had received reports that Fitz Lee's and Wade Hampton's cavalry had captured a sizeable number of prisoners in an engagement. As a result, Early thought that it would be "better to go by Louisa Court-House and try and smash up Sheridan and

then turn off to Charlottesville," for he feared that if "he is near, my trains will not be safe." *Official Records*, LI, pt. 2, pp. 1012-1013.

2. Jubal A. Early, *Narrative of the War Between the States* (Repr.: New York, 1989), p. 380.

3. Major General Lewis "Lew" Wallace was born in Indiana. He participated in the capture of Fort Donelson and earned the rank of major general. At Shiloh he bungled an opportunity in smashing General Albert Sidney Johnston's left flank. In March 1864, despite objections from Halleck, he was assigned to command of the VIII Army Corps and the Middle Department. After the war he became well known as the author of *Ben Hur*.

   With Early's advance through western Maryland Wallace led a smaller army to Frederick to determine the size of the Southern force. He established his headquarters at Monocacy Junction to contest Early's move and to determine his objective. On the Monocacy River, with few fords along the river and its high bluff to the east of it, Wallace's position was strong. The Junction also had additional strategic value. The railroad with its link to Harper's Ferry would maintain communication with the garrison there. In addition the two turnpikes leading to Baltimore and Washington were close by. They provided avenues of retreat, if necessary, but more important in case of a Confederate victory would expose the route and objective of the Southern army. Richard R. Duncan, "Maryland's Reaction to Early's Raid in 1864: A Summer of Bitterness," *Maryland Historical Magazine* (Fall, 1969), vol. 64, pp. 254-255. For a biographical treatment of Wallace see Robert E. Morsberger and Katharine M. Morsberger, *Lew Wallace: Militant Romantic* (New York: McGraw-Hill Book Company, 1980); for Wallace in Maryland and Monocacy see chpts. 10 & 11.

   For an excellent account of the Battle of Monocacy and Confederate movements in western Maryland see B. F. Cooling, *Jubal Early's Raid on Washington 1864* (Baltimore, 1989); also see Millard Kessler Bushong, *Old Jube* (Shippensburg, Pa.: White Mane Publishing Co., 1990; and Glenn H. Worthington, *Fighting for Time* (Shippensburg, Pa.: Burd Street Press, 1985).

4. Major General Philip Henry Sheridan, a West Point graduate of the class of 1853, served in the West until 1864. Ultimately he came to the attention of General U. S. Grant in the battle of Chattanooga. Grant in the spring of that year placed him in charge of the cavalry of the Army of the Potomac, and despite a mixed record of victories and reverses his reputation was considerably enhanced. Ultimately, he was placed in command of Federal forces combatting Early. See Warner, *Generals in Blue*, pp. 437-439.

5. *Official Records*, XXXVII, pt. 2, p. 558 and XLIII, pt. 1, pp. 697-698; Grant, *Memoirs*, II, app., pp. 581-582.

6. Kershaw's division was commanded by Major General Joseph Brevard Kershaw. Colonel Wilfred E. Cutshaw, commander of Cutshaw's battalion of artillery, was attached to the division in the Valley campaign under Early.

   In early September Kershaw, whose division had joined Early in mid-August, was ordered to return to Lee's army. Sheridan had shrewdly secured an intelligence contact in Winchester, and when Kershaw's division left on September 15, Miss Rebecca Wright, a young Quaker Unionist, sent word of it to the general by a black courier. For Sheridan, "Miss Wright's answer proved of more value to me than she anticipated . . . and this circumstance led, three days later, to the battle of the Opequon, or Winchester as it has been unofficially called." Philip H. Sheridan, *Personal Memoirs of P. H. Sheridan* (New York, 1888), II, pp. 3-9; D. Augustus Dickert, *History of Kershaw's Brigade* (Dayton, Ohio, 1976, p. 435.

7. Colonel James A. Mulligan of Mulligan's Separate Brigade, 23rd Illinois Infantry.
   With reports indicating that a Confederate army was advancing down the Valley, Sigel ordered the stores at Martinsburg to be sent to Harper's Ferry for safety. He hoped that General Sullivan's Division would soon arrive at Martinsburg, for, as he informed the War Department, he had only two regiments and a battery there to defend the town. Finally, in evacuating the town, he withdrew to Harper's Ferry and on his arrival there the garrison under General Max Weber and his forces crossed over the river to Maryland Heights. Franz Sigel to Adjutant General of the Army, July 2 & 5, 1864, Box #5, folder 2, Sigel Papers.
   From early July until early September Confederate forces intermittently wrecked and controlled the railroad. The Baltimore and Ohio sustained heavy losses during this period. With the movement of Early's army eastward into western Maryland and towards Washington the company enjoyed a brief respite and repaired the line quickly. By June 21 trains again moved along the line. However, with the return of the Confederate army to the Valley Southern destruction of the railroad rendered large stretches inoperative. It was not until mid-September when Sheridan forced Early to withdraw towards Winchester that the railroad was again in operation. Festus P. Summers, *The Baltimore and Ohio in the Civil War* (New York, 1939), pp. 123-124.

8. The region was suffering from an "unprecedented drought." Navigation on the river was difficult even on those with a shallow draught. David H. Strother, "Operations in West Virginia," in Frank Moore, *Rebellion Record*, XI, p. 488.

9. The official report of losses covering the period between June 10 and 23 was given as 940 killed, wounded, and captured or missing. *Official Records*, XXXVII, pt. 1, pp. 103-106.

10. From Charleston, West Virginia, Colonel Rutherford B. Hayes, writing to his mother on June 30 and referring to the army's affection and confidence in General Crook, wrote, "General Hunter is not so fortunate." Two days later he reiterated that same sentiment in another letter to her, "General Hunter *was* chief in command, and is not much esteemed by us. . . ." Williams, *Diary and Letters of Hayes*, II, pp. 478 & 480.

11. Early's army consisted of approximately 10,000 infantry and 4,000 cavalry and artillery. Jubal Early, *War Memoirs; Autobiographical Sketch and Narrative of the War between the States* (Repr.: Bloomington, Ind., 1960); Freeman, *Lee's Lieutenants*, III, p. 558.

12. A sizeable quantity of ammunition, valued at some 3 million dollars for Hunter's army, was at the depot there. A great effort was made to ship it and other stores to safety. Sigel ordered J. W. Garrett, President of the Baltimore and Ohio Railroad, to send 150 railroad cars to Martinsburg to carry away as much of the government supplies there as possible. However, those stores and private baggage which could not be saved were burned as Sigel's men evacuated Martinsburg. D. J. Young to Franz Sigel, July 6 and Sigel to the adjutant general of U.S. Army, July 6, 1864, Box 5, folder 2, Sigel Papers; *Official Records*, XXXVII, pt. 2, p. 16.

13. Hunter had James E. Wharton, editor of the Parkersburg *Gazette*, arrested and the paper suspended. The general denied that it was in retaliation for Wharton's criticism of his handling of the Lynchburg campaign. In reply to a letter of enquiry by Governor Boreman of West Virginia, Hunter charged that the editor had published contraband information in reporting that his army had passed through Parkersburg on its way to the East, which he maintained was not true. Actually Wharton, a Unionist, had already been released by the time of the receipt of the governor's letter. In the controversy Grant defended Hunter to the War Department. On July 15 he wrote C. A. Dana, assistant secretary of war, that "If Gen. Hunter has made war upon the newspapers of West Va probably

he has done right." Baltimore, *American and Commercial Advertiser*, July 22, 1864; Simon, *Grant Papers*, vol. 11, p. 251.

As to the charge that Hunter horsewhipped a soldier, Grant indicated to Dana that "he has laid himself subject to trial but nine chances out of ten he has only acted on the spur of the moment under great provocation." Simon, *Grant Papers*, vol. 11, pp. 251 & 251-252n.

14. Major General Horatio G. Wright, commanding the VI Corps, was placed in charge of Federal forces pursuing Early in his retreat back into Virginia. Hunter was left in charge of the Department of West Virginia, but Crook was assigned immediate command of his units. Hunter was furious and offered his resignation. Lincoln, in attempting to conciliate him, declined to accept it. *Official Records*, XXXVII, pt. 2, pp. 315-316, 339-342; Roy P. Basler, ed., *Collected Works of Abraham Lincoln* (New Brunswick, N.J., 1953), VII, p. 445.

15. For an account of the battle see Peter J. Meaney, O.S.B., *The Civil War Engagement at Cool Spring July 18, 1864* (Berryville, Va., 1980). Neil's estimate of the size of Early's army was considerably exaggerated. Federal casualties of killed, wounded, and missing were estimated at 442. Confederate figures are impossible to determine and estimates vary from 200 to 600. Meaney feels that the best estimate would be around 400. See Meaney, *Cool Spring*, app. A, p. 54.

16. Neil's information and estimate of Early's army was grossly exaggerated. Early concentrated his army near Middletown, and on July 24 he struck at General Crook's army at Kernstown. The attack drove the Federals through Winchester and forced Crook to retreat across the Potomac River. Early, *Memoirs*, pp. 398-400; Schmitt, *General George Crook*, p. 123; Freeman, *Lee's Lieutenants*, p. 571, and Bushong, *Old Jube*, pp. 212-214.

17. Neil's figures are exaggerated. Early estimated that his forces captured only 200 to 300 prisoners. His loss in the battle was slight. Early, *Narrative*, p. 400.

18. In a Confederate cavalry raid General John McCausland's men crossed the Potomac River into western Maryland and southern Pennsylvania on July 29 to strike at Chambersburg. Other Southern cavalry units demonstrated against Federal positions at Harper's Ferry, Hagerstown, and other points. McCausland, creating panic in the region, reached Chambersburg on the morning of July 30.

19. The 1860 population of Frederick was 8,143.

20. Mayor William G. Cole was brought to the city hall where he was presented with a demand for $200,000 to insure the safety of the city. The mayor immediately assembled a meeting of the remaining city council members and a group of prominent citizens to discuss the ransom. An attempt was made to have the sum reduced, but the request was rejected. They were informed that if it were not paid, the Confederates would help themselves. Frederick *Maryland Union*, July 21, 1864.

21. Angered over reports that Southern sympathizers aided Early, Hunter ordered the arrest of all persons and their families who had pointed out Union property or had given other such information to the Confederates. The order was suspended by Lincoln. *Official Records*, XXXVII, pt. 2, p. 378; Frederick *Examiner*, Aug. 10, 1864; Duncan, "Maryland's Reaction to Early's Raid," pp. 277-279.

22. In retaliation for Hunter's depredations in northern Virginia, Jefferson County and other such acts in the South, Early decided that "it was time to open the eyes of the people of the North to this enormity, by an example in the way of retaliation." He selected Chambersburg for the lesson. In the proclamation of justification, Early specifically cited the burning of the homes of Andrew Hunter, A. R. Boteler, E. J. Lee, Governor Letcher, J. T. Anderson and the Virginia Military Institute. Early sent two cavalry brigades and a battery of artillery under General John McCausland on the punitive expedition. Reaching the town, McCausland demanded a ransom of "$100,000 in gold or $500,000 in current Northern funds" under threat of burning the town. After waiting six hours without receiving the

required money, the Confederates began the destruction. In carrying out the orders McCausland later wrote, "The wanton destruction of private property of citizens of Virginia by orders of General Hunter . . . may be considered as one of the strongest reasons for the retaliation by Early's orders upon the city of Chambersburg." Early, *Memoirs*, p. 401; John McCausland, "The Burning of Chambersburg, Penn." *S.H.S.P.*, vol. 31, pp. 266-270; Henry Kyd Douglas, *I Rode with Stonewall* (Chapel Hill, N.C., 1940), p. 303; Bushong, *Old Jube*, pp. 222-226.

23. Frustrated with the situation in the Valley, Grant, after being denied his first choice, wanted General Philip H. Sheridan placed in "command of all troops in the field" and "to put himself south of the enemy and follow him to the death. Wherever the enemy goes let our troops go also." Lincoln saw the dispatch to Halleck and fully approved. However, he warned Grant that "it will neither be done nor attempted unless you watch it every day, and hour, and force." Grant went to Monocacy Junction to confer with Hunter. Believing that he no longer enjoyed the confidence of the administration, Hunter asked to be relieved of command. The two, at Grant's request, were soon joined by Sheridan, who assumed command on August 7. *Official Records*, XXXVIII, pt. 2, pp. 1, 558, 572, 582, and XLII, pt. 1, pp. 726, 747, 962; Basler, *Works of Lincoln*, VII, p. 476; Grant, *Memoirs*, II, pp. 317-321; and Richard O'Connor, *Sheridan the Inevitable* (Indianapolis, Ind., 1953), pp. 190-193.

24. The War Department on August 7 created the Middle Military Division under the command of General Sheridan. The Division consisted of the departments of Washington, Susquehanna, West Virginia, and the Middle Department. *Official Records*, XLIII, pt. 1, 79 & 721.

25. Present day Stephen City. Initially Early was camped there, but on the 12th he had moved to Hupp's Hill. When he found that the Federals were moving towards him with a larger force than anticipated, he retired to Fisher's Hill, slightly south of Strasburg. There he intended to await Sheridan's attack. Instead, on the morning of the 17th Early found that the Federals were withdrawing. Early, *Memoirs*, pp. 406-407.

26. Concerned about the Federal build-up in the Harper's Ferry area, Lee detached Lieutenant General Richard H. Anderson, who was temporarily commanding Longstreet's Corps while he recuperated from a wound suffered at the battle of Wilderness, from his corps to go to Early's aid. Kershaw's Division and initially Major Wade Hampton's cavalry were placed under him. Anderson's independent command was to operate east of the Blue Ridge Mountains but moved temporarily into the Valley to help Early in his ceaseless maneuvering to create an illusion of growing Confederate strength. Anderson's detachment from his corps without sending it with him was done intentionally to add to the impression of sizeable reinforcements being sent to the Valley. With Sheridan's lack of boldness and Early's increasing overconfidence, Kershaw's Division and Anderson were ordered to return to Lee's Army of Northern Virginia in the middle of September. The decision gave Sheridan his long awaited opportunity to attack Early. Dowdey, *Wartime Papers of R. E. Lee*, pp. 832-835; Freeman, *Lee's Lieutenants*, III, pp. 574-576; Joseph Cantey Elliot, *Lieutenant General Richard Heron Anderson: Lee's Noble Soldier* (Dayton, Ohio, 1985), pp. 111-112.

Neil's figures on the strength of both armies were greatly exaggerated. Longstreet had not reinforced the Second Corps. Early estimated he "had about 8,500 muskets for duty." Early, *Narrative*, pp. 415-416.

27. It was Massanutten Mountain. William Hewitt estimated the loss at three of four killed or wounded. Hewitt, *History of the Twelfth Regiment*, pp. 171-172.

28. Sheridan's men constructed breast works of fence rails and railroad ties and other material stretching from the Potomac to the Shenandoah rivers. Hewitt, *History of the Twelfth Regiment*, p. 173.

29. Neil's father was nominated as a candidate for auditor of Delaware County, Ohio.

30. The skirmishing lasted for three days. Finally, the Confederate line was broken, and the Southerners retreated to the Stephenson Depot vicinity. Hewitt, *History of Twelfth Regiment*, p. 173.

31. On August 24 a concentration of Confederate infantry prepared to attack Federal troops who were destroying the Weldon Railroad. Skirmishing broke out near Reams' Station. Hancock's II Corps was defeated in a surprise attack by A. P. Hill's strengthened corps.

32. Anderson had hoped to surprise a Federal force at Berryville. On the morning of September 3 he sent Fitz Lee's cavalry to reconnoiter. Then he sent for Kershaw's Division. The surprise turned out to be for Anderson. Unexpectedly, he ran into the VIII Corps. In a bluff he attacked the Federals on both their flanks, forcing them to retreat. Elliott, *General Richard Heron Anderson*, pp. 113-115.

33. General George B. McClellan was nominated by the Democratic party in Chicago as its presidential candidate in 1864 on a platform that asserted that the war was a failure and called "for a cessation of hostilities with a view to an ultimate convention of the States or other peaceable means." In his acceptance letter McClellan virtually repudiated the plank. Eugene H. Roseboom, *A History of Presidential Elections* (New York, 1957), pp. 198-201.

34. The reference is to the Opequon Creek.

35. Skirmish rather than a battle.

36. During Early's attack on Crook at Kernstown on July 24 Colonel Curtis was separated from his regiment. He finally returned on the 26th. Hewitt, *Twelfth West Virginia*, p. 163.

37. Skirmishing erupted on the fords of the Opequon Creek, Bunker Hill, and near Berryville. E. B. Long, *The Civil War Day By Day: An Almanac 1861-1865* (Garden City, N.Y., 1971). p. 569.

38. On the eve of the battle of Winchester Early's strength was estimated at 8,500 infantry, 750 artillery, and 2,900 cavalry for a total of 12,150 men. Early, *War Memoirs*, pp. 415-416; Bushong, *Old Jube*, p. 232.

39. For the battles at Winchester and Fisher's Hill see Jeffry D. Wert, *From Winchester to Cedar Creek: The Shenandoah Campaign of 1864* (Carlisle, Pa., 1987) and Thomas A. Lewis, *The Guns of Cedar Creek* (New York, 1988).

40. Early estimated his losses at Winchester at 3,611 killed, wounded and missing. This did not include cavalry losses which Douglas Southall Freeman in *Lee's Lieutenants* estimated at 1,000. At Fisher's Hill Early reported 1,235 killed, wounded and missing. E. B. Long in *The Civil War Day By Day* cites the casualty figures as: Federal, 697 dead, 2,983 wounded, 338 missing [Total 4,018]; Confederate, 276 dead, 1,827 wounded, captured or missing 1,818 [Total 3,921]. Bushong, *Old Jube*, pp. 236, 242; Freeman, *Lee's Lieutenants*, III, p. 581; Long, *Civil War Day By Day*, p. 571.

41. In a flanking movement on the Southern left flank near North Mountain the Federals struck a telling blow at Early's position. His whole line gave way in confusion. Early reported the loss of twelve pieces of artillery. *Official Records*, XLIII, pt. 1, p. 557. E. B. Long cites the casualty figures as: Federal, 528; Confederates, 1,235 dead, wounded, and missing. Long, *Civil War Day By Day*, p. 573; McDonald, *Make Me a Map*, p. 230.

42. Confederate losses included Major General Robert Emmett Rodes who was mortally wounded. For the Union, Brigadier General David Allen Russell was killed, while Generals Upton Emory, John Baillie McIntosh, and Edward Payson Chapman were wounded. Warner, *Generals in Gray*, p. 263, and *Generals in Blue*, pp. 80-81, 300-301, 416-417, 519-520; Edward J. Stackpole, *Sheridan in the Shenandoah: Jubal Early's Nemesis* (Harrisburg, Pa., 1961), p. 238.

43. As Sheridan prepared to pull back to Cedar Creek from Harrisonburg, skirmishing broke out at Bridgewater and Mount Crawford. Long, *Civil War Day By Day*, pp. 577-578.

44. Colonel Rutherford B. Hayes on October 2 noted at Harrisonburg, "A hegira of Dunkards and others." Williams, *Diary and Letters of Hayes*, II, p. 520.

45. Lieutenant John R. Meigs, son of the quartermaster general, graduated first in his class at West Point in June 1863 and received his commission as a second lieutenant in the Corps of Engineers. Under Sheridan he became chief engineer of the Army of the Shenandoah. Russell F. Weigley, *Quartermaster General of the Union Army: A Biography of M. C. Meigs* (New York, 1959). pp. 302-307.

     Sheridan, believing that Meigs had been killed by bushwhackers, was furious. In retaliation he ordered the burning of houses within a five mile radius. After watching the burning of some houses in the small village of Dayton, Sheridan called a halt to it. Instead, he ordered the arrest of all able-bodied men in the area. Meanwhile during the night, the citizens of Dayton camped out in the adjacent fields waiting for Sheridan's order to be carried out on the next morning. They were greatly relieved when it was rescinded. Sheridan, *Personal Memoirs*, II, pp. 50-52; O'Connor, *Sheridan*, p. 214; Carrie B. Sites and Effie A. Hess, eds., *A History of the Town of Dayton Virginia* (Berryville, Va.), p. 67.

46. Dr. George C. Gans.

47. In November 1862 Jackson ordered General D. H. Hill's division to destroy the Manassas Gap Railroad from Strasburg to Mount Jackson. Angus James Johnston II, *Virginia Railroads in the Civil War* (Chapel Hill, N.C., 1961), p. 113.

48. The Confederate cavalry under Generals Thomas Rosser and Lumsford Lomax clashed with Generals George A. Custer's and Wesley Merritt's cavalry at Tom's Brook on the 9th. Southern daring in a classic cavalry battle turned into a disaster for them. The Confederates lost eleven valuable guns. Freeman, *Lee's Lieutenants*, III, pp. 596-597; Sheridan, *Personal Memoirs*, II, 56-58; Jeffry Wert, "The Woodstock Races," *Civil War Times Illustrated*, XIX (May, 1980), pp. 8-12, 38-40; and O'Connor, *Sheridan*, p. 216.

49. Lieutenant Colonel Tolles, chief quartermaster, and Dr. Ohlenschalager were mortally wounded in the attack by a band of guerrillas. The initial report indicated that four had been killed and five or six wounded. *Official Records*, XLIII, pt. 2, p. 351.

50. The information on the shooting was probably confused with Sheridan's order following the death of Lieutenant Meigs. Tolles' death, however, increased Sheridan's anger over the activities of partisan bands behind his lines. On November 12 he ordered Merritt to ferret out Mosby in Loundon County and in doing so "clear the country of forage and subsistence, so as to prevent the guerrillas from being harbored there in the future...." Sheridan, *Personal Memoirs*, pp. 99-100.

51. A detachment of some 120 Mosby rangers under Sam Chapman, initially intending to attack a Federal picket post at Chester Gap, struck instead at a wagon train near Front Royal on September 22. Quickly, it became obvious that the attack was a mistake, for the train was escorted by some 200 Federals. In the skirmish Lieutenant Charles McMaster was killed. Federals charged that McMaster had been killed after attempting to surrender. Custer was furious. Four Southerners were shot and two hanged. Mosby, confining his anger to Custer's and Powell's units, retaliated in kind and executed seven Federals. Mosby sent a message to Sheridan on November 11 that he would treat "any prisoners falling into my hands . . . with kindness," unless, as he threatened, "some new act of barbarity shall compel me reluctantly to adopt a line of policy repugnant to humanity." Virgil Carrington Jones, *Ranger Mosby* (Chapel Hill, N.C., 1944), pp. 207-228.

52. In the October state elections the Union party carried Ohio by a 54,000 major-
    ity. Out of the nineteen Congressional seats Unionists won seventeen. George
    H. Porter, *Ohio Politics During the Civil War Period* (Repr.: New York, 1968), pp.
    125-126.
53. Federal losses were estimated at 644 killed, 3,430 wounded, 1,591 missing for
    a total of 5,665. Confederate loss, estimated by Livermore, was 320 killed,
    1,540 wounded, and 1,050 missing, for a total of 2,910. *Official Records*, XLIII,
    pt. 1, pp. 131-137; Livermore, *Numbers & Losses*, pp. 129-130.
54. Early reported to Lee on October 20 and 21 that he had lost 23 pieces of artil-
    lery. Sheridan, on the other hand, reported having captured 48 pieces, at least
    300 wagons and ambulances and 1,600 prisoners. *Official Records*, XLIII, pt. 1,
    pp. 424, 436-437, 560-564.
55. Following the Battle of Cedar Creek, the largest Federal hospital under one
    authority during the war was established at Winchester. Consisting of tents, it
    housed some 4,000 wounded. However, as a model, George Washington Adams
    points out, "As the surgeon commanding it found himself so immersed in pa-
    per work that he could carry on no ward inspection, the experiment can hardly
    be called a success." Adams, *Doctors in Blue*, pp. 99-100.
56. Sheridan had been called to Washington for consultations. On returning to the
    Valley he spent the night of October 18 at Winchester before continuing to the
    front. Early on the morning of the 19th, Sheridan was awakened by an officer
    who reported "irregular and fitful" artillery firing coming from the South. Later,
    as he was leaving Winchester, he heard the "unceasing roar" of artillery and
    soon encountered fleeing soldiers. Hurrying to the front, he found Wright's VI
    Corps holding fast. However, Sheridan's appearance was an important psycho-
    logical tonic for the Union army and helped to change the tide of battle from
    possible defeat to an aggressive counterattack and victory. Sheridan, *Personal
    Memoirs*, II, pp. 64-92; *Official Records*, XLIII, pt. 1, pp. 32-34, and pt. 2, pp. 410,
    424, 436-437; O'Connor, *Sheridan*, pp. 217-231.
57. Brigadier General Alfred Napoleon Alexander Duffie was captured on October
    24 by Mosby near Winchester. He was later paroled in February and exchanged
    in April 1865. The incident ended his military career. Sheridan in a dispatch to
    Halleck summed him up, "I think him a trifling man and a poor soldier. He was
    captured by his own stupidity." Quoted in Virgil Carrington Jones, *Gray Ghosts
    and Rebel Raiders* (McLean, Virginia: EPM Publications, Inc., 1984), p. 319; Warner,
    Generals in Blue, pp. 131-132; Jones, *Ranger Mosby*, p. 221.
58. Early's army moved down the Valley on November 10. Rosser's command was
    on the left, moving to Fairview, and continued on the Back Road to the west of
    Newtown. Custer struck at a portion of Rosser's brigade and drove it back
    until reinforcements were brought up. McDonald, *Make Me a Map*, pp. 242-243.
         Rosser proved to be a feisty leader in the Valley. As Gregory J. W. Urwin
    points out, "There was one Confederate officer in the valley who never learned
    the meaning of the word *quit*—Thomas Lafayette Rosser." Despite being de-
    feated by Custer in a number of engagements, he refused to give up. Gregory
    J. W. Urwin, *Custer Victorious* (East Brunswick, N.J., 1983), p. 219.
59. See Baltimore, *American and Commercial Advertiser*, Nov. 3, 1864.
60. The repair of the railroad became a special target for Mosby's men. The pros-
    pect of its repair was one of the reasons for Early's move back down the Valley
    on November 10. With the changed conditions in the Valley Federal authorities
    abandoned the idea of restoring it to use. Jeffry D. Wert, *Mosby's Rangers* (New
    York, 1990), pp. 225-236; Early, *Memoirs*, p. 453.
61. Neil's information was confused and inaccurate. "Kenilworth," among the more
    notable estates in Frederick County, was owned by the Stephenson family. At
    William Stephenson's death in 1857 he left it as a life estate for his wife and
    then at her death to his son, Henry. Henry held title to it until his death in 1904.

Garland R. Quarles, *Some Old Homes in Frederick County, Virginia* (Quarles, 1971), pp. 191-192; T. K. Cartmell, *Shenandoah Valley Pioneers and Their Descendants* (Berryville, Va., 1963), p. 482.

62. Thomas L. Rosser, in leading an expedition against the Baltimore and Ohio Railroad, clashed with a small Federal force near Moorefield on November 27. After capturing 40 prisoners and an artillery piece, the Confederates struck at New Creek and Piedmont on the following day. They captured Fort Kelley, 700 prisoners, 4 field pieces and 4 siege guns and destroyed considerable government property. *Official Records*, XLIII, pt. 1, pp. 653-670.

63. Brigadier General George Henry Thomas was then defending Nashville against General John B. Hood's army.

64. Washington constructed the fort in 1757 during the French and Indian War. Morton, *Story of Winchester in Virginia*, pp. 73-74.

65. Thomas Lord Fairfax, Baron of Cameron, as sole heir to a grant made originally by Charles II to Lord Culpeper and his associates, was the proprietor of the Northern Neck of Virginia in the late Colonial period. Ibid, pp. 28-30.

66. Early attempted to reorganize his command at New Market. There his infantry rested for the remainder of October. His cavalry under General Lunsford Lomax repulsed Brigadier General William H. Powell's troops in the Luray Valley. In November Early, believing that Sheridan was sending troops to Grant, moved his small army down the Valley towards Middletown. Sheridan, using his cavalry under Custer, Merritt, and Powell struck at Early and forced him back to New Market. There Kershaw's division was returned to Lee and General G. B. Cosby's men were sent back to southwest Virginia. Later at Waynesboro on March 2 Sheridan completely shattered Early's remaining army. Bushong, *Old Jube*, pp. 266-267 & 277-280; See Early, *Memoirs*, chpt. L.

67. Probably Edward C. Jolliffe who lived at Clear Brook, a few miles to the north of Stephenson on the Valley Pike.

68. In a two day battle before Nashville, the Army of the Cumberland under George Thomas shattered Hood's Army of Tennessee on December 16.

69. Brigadier General Thomas Maley Harris commanded a brigade under Crook. He was made a brevet brigadier general following the Battle of Cedar Creek and on March 29, 1865, was promoted to full rank. Warner, *Generals in Blue*, p. 210.

EPILOGUE

1. Neil to Father & Mother, Dec. 25, 1864, Neil Papers.
2. Neil to Father & Mother, Jan. 4, 1865, ibid.
3. Neil to Father & Mother, Feb. 21, 1865, ibid. On his trip back to the front Neil stopped in Wheeling and saw both Governor Boreman and Adjutant General Pierpont "who seemed glad to see me." At Washington he paid a visit to his cousin James Sidney Rollins of Columbia, Missouri, member of the House of Representatives from July 4, 1861, to March 3, 1865. Ibid., Feb. 11, 1864; Ben: Perley Poore, *The Political Register and Congressional Directory* (Boston, 1878), p. 603.
4. Neil to Father & Mother, Feb. 21 & March 7, 1865, ibid.
5. Special Orders No. 3, issued on January 4, provided amnesty and transportation to areas behind Northern lines and payment for surrendering their weapons and other property for Confederate deserters on taking an oath of allegiance. *Official Records*, XLVI, pt. 2, pp. 828-829; Neil to Father & Mother, March 4, 1865, Neil Papers.
6. Neil to Father & Mother, March 4 & 12 & April 1, 1865, Neil Papers. See Cresap, *Appomattox Commander*, Chpt. 12 for the XXIV Corps' role in the campaign.
7. See Appendix A.

8. Neil to Dear Friends, April 21, 1865, Neil Papers.
9. The second Wheeling convention declared that the officials in Richmond had abrogated their authority by their disloyal actions. The delegates then organized a loyal state government and elected Francis H. Pierpont governor. On May 9, 1865, President Andrew Johnson appointed Pierpont Provisional Governor of Virginia. He was subject to military authority, and Pierpont returned to Richmond to re-establish the state government.
10. Lincoln was assassinated on April 14, 1865, in Ford's Theater in Washington.
11. Neil to Dear Friends, April 26, 1865, Neil Papers.
12. Neil to Friends, April 26 & 29, 1865, ibid.
13. Neil to Friends, May 8 & 12, 1865, ibid.
14. Neil to Friends, May 12 & June 7 & 12, 1865, ibid.
15. Neil to Dear People and Friends, June 14 & 22, 1865, ibid.

Selected Bibliography

Manuscripts

John T. Booth Papers, 1861–1865, Ohio Historical Society.
Diary of James F. Ellis, Roy Bird Cook Collection, West Virginia University.
Diary of William M. Goudy, Civil War Diaries Collection, West Virginia University.
Russell Hastings Papers, Rutherford B. Hayes Library, Fremont, Ohio.
Milton W. Humphreys Diary, University of Virginia, Charlottesville, Virginia.
Alexander Neil Papers, University of Virginia, Charlottesville, Virginia.
William Patterson Diary, Southern Historical Collection, University of North Carolina.
Franz Sigel Papers, Western Reserve Historical Society, Cleveland, Ohio.

Documents, Memoirs, Published Diaries and Letters

Basler, Roy P., ed. *Collected Works of Abraham Lincoln.* 9 vols. New Brunswick, N.J.: Rutgers University Press, 1953.
Douglas, Henry Kyd. *I Rode With Stonewall.* Chapel Hill, N.C.: The University of North Carolina Press, 1940.
Early, Jubal. *A Memoir of the Last Year of the War for Independence.* Lynchburg, Va.: Charles W. Button, 1867.
Early, Jubal. *War Memoirs: Autobiographical Sketch and Narrative of the War between the States.* Repr., Bloomington, Ind.: Indiana University Press, 1960.
Eby, Cecil D., Jr., ed. *A Virginia Yankee in the Civil War: The Diaries of David Hunter Strother.* Chapel Hill, N.C.: The University of North Carolina Press, 1961.

Eckert, Edward K. and Nicholas J. Amato, ed. *Ten years in the Saddle: The Memoir of William Woods Averell.* San Rafael, Calif.: Presidio Press, 1978.

Grant, Ulysses S. *Personal Memoirs of U. S. Grant.* Repr., New York: Bonanza Books.

Hunter, David. *Report of the Military Services of Gen. David Hunter, U.S.A.* New York: D. Van Nostrand, 1873.

Imboden, J. D. "Fire, Sword, and the Halter," in *Annals of the War* (Philadelphia: The Times Publishing Company, 1879), pp. 169–183.

Journal of American Medical Association, vol. 36 (Chicago, 1901).

Kennedy, Jos. C. G. *Preliminary Report on The Eighth Census, 1860.* Washington: Government Printing Office, 1862.

McCausland, John. "The Burning of Chambersburg, Penn.", *Southern Historical Society Papers,* vol. 31, pp. 266–270.

Medical College of Ohio. *Annual Announcement of Lectures for the Session of 1863–4 and Catalogue of Students and Graduates for the Sessions of 1862–3.* Cincinnati, 1863.

Moore, Frank, ed. *The Rebellion Record.* 11 vols. New York: D. Van Nostrand, 1864–1868.

O'Reilly, Miles. *Baked Meats of the Funeral.* New York: Carleton, 1866.

Report of the Proceedings in the Case of the United States vs Charles J. Guiteau. Washington, 1882.

Russell, Charles Wells, ed. *Memoirs of Colonel John S. Mosby.* Bloomington, Ind.: Indiana University Press, 1959.

Schmitt, Martin F., ed. *General George Crook; His Autobiography.* Norman, Okla.: University of Oklahoma Press, 1986.

Sheridan, Philip. *Personal Memoirs of Philip Sheridan, General of United States Army.* New York: D. Appleton and Company, 1902.

Sigel, Franz. "Sigel in the Shenandoah Valley in 1864," in *Battles and Leaders of the Civil War* (Repr., New York: Thomas Yoseloff, 1959), IV, pp. 487–491.

Simon, John Y., ed. *The Papers of Ulysses S. Grant.* 20 vols. Carbondale, Ill.: Southern Illinois University Press, 1967–.

Strother, David. "Operations in West Virginia: Report of Colonel Strother," in Frank Moore, ed., *The Rebellion Record: A Diary of American Events.* New York: D. Van Nostrand, 1864–68.

Thirty-Sixth Announcement of Lectures of the Medical College of Ohio for the Session of 1855–1856. Cincinnati, 1855.

Turner, Charles W., Jr., ed. "General David Hunter's Sack of Lexington, Virginia, June 10–15, 1864; An account by Rose Page Pendleton," *Virginia Magazine of History and Biography* (April, 1975), vol. 83, pp. 173–183.

U.S. War Department. *The War of the Rebellion: A Compilation of the Official Records of the Union and Confederate Armies.* 128 vols. Washington, D.C.: Government Printing Office, 1880–1901.

Williams, Charles Richard, ed. *Diary and Letters of Rutherford B. Hayes.* 4 vols. Columbus: The Ohio State Archeological and Historical Society, 1922.

Directories

Atkinson, William B., ed. *The Physicians and Surgeons of the United States.* Philadelphia: Charles Robson, 1878.

Livermore, Thomas L. *Numbers & Losses in the Civil War.* Bloomington, Ind.: Indiana University Press, 1957.

Ben: Perley Poore. *The Political Register and Congressional Directory.* Boston, 1878.

Warner, Ezra J. *Generals in Blue.* Baton Rouge, La.: Louisiana State University Press, 1964.

Warner, Ezra J. *Generals in Gray.* Baton Rouge, La.: Louisiana State University Press, 1959.

Watson, Irving. *A Physicians and Surgeons of America.* Concord, New Hampshire: Republican Press Association, 1896.

Newspapers

Baltimore, *American and Commercial Advertiser.*
Columbus, Ohio *Dispatch.*
Frederick, Maryland *Examiner.*
Frederick, Maryland *Maryland Union.*
Richmond, *Richmond Whig.*
Wheeling, West Virginia, *Daily Intelligencer.*

Regimental and Campaign Studies

Beach, William H. *The First New York (Lincoln) Cavalry.* New York: The Lincoln Cavalry Association, 1902.

Blackford, Charles M. *The Campaign and Battle of Lynchburg.* Lynchburg, Va.: J. P. Ben Co., 1907.

Brice, Marshall Moore. *Conquest of a Valley.* Verona, Va.: University Press of Virginia, 1963.

Cooling, Benjamin F. *Jubal Early's Raid on Washington 1864.* Baltimore: Nautical & Aviation Publishing Company of America, 1989.

Davis, William C. *The Battle of New Market.* Baton Rouge, La.: Louisiana State University Press, 1975.

Delauter, Roger U., Jr. *The 18th Virginia Cavalry.* Lynchburg, Va.: H. E. Howard, Inc., 1985.

Delauter, Roger U., Jr. *McNeill's Rangers.* Lynchburg, Va.: H. E. Howard, Inc., 1986.

Du Pont, Henry A. *The Campaign of 1864 in the Valley of Virginia and Expedition to Lynchburg.* New York: National Americana Society, 1925.

Hewitt, William. *History of the Twelfth West Virginia Infantry.* Published by the Twelfth West Virginia Volunteer Infantry Association.

Humphreys, Milton W. *A History of the Lynchburg Campaign.* Charlottesville, Va.: Michie Company, 1924.

Lewis, Thomas A. *The Guns of Cedar Creek*. New York: Harper & Row, Publishers, 1988.

Lincoln, William S. *Life with the Thirty-Fourth Massachusetts Infantry in the War of the Rebellion*. Worcester, Mass.: Press of Noyes, Snow & Company, 1879.

Lynch, Charles H. *The Civil War Diary*. Privately Printed, 1915.

Meaney, Peter J., O.S.B. *The Civil War Engagement at Cool Spring July 18, 1864*. Berryville, Va.: Proceedings of the Clark County Historical Association, 1980.

Nye, Wilburg Sturtevant. *Here Come the Rebels!* Baton Rouge, La.: Louisiana State University Press, 1965.

Reader, Frank S. *History of the Fifth West Virginia Cavalry*. Brighton, Pa.: Frank S. Reader, 1890.

Vandiver, Frank. *Jubal's Raid: General Early's Famous Attack on Washington in 1864*. New York: McGraw-Hill Book Company, Inc., 1960.

Wert, Jeffry D. *From Winchester to Cedar Creek: The Shenandoah Campaign of 1864*. Carlisle, Pa.: South Mountain Press, Inc., Publishers, 1987.

Wildes, Thos. F. *Record of the One Hundred and Sixteenth Regiment Ohio Infantry Volunteers*. Sandusky, Ohio: I. F. Mack & Bro., 1884.

Books

A Centennial Biographical History of the City of Columbus and Franklin County Ohio. Chicago, 1901.

Adams, George Washington. *Doctors in Blue*. New York: Collier Books, 1961.

Aler, Vernon. *Aler's History of Martinsburg an Berkeley County, West Virginia*. Hagerstown, Md.: The Mail Publishing Company, 1888.

Bushong, Millard K. *Old Jube*. [Boyce, Va.: Carr Publishing Company, Inc., 1955.] Shippensburg, Pa.: White Mane Publishing Co., Inc., 1990.

Cartmell, T. M. *Shenandoah Valley Pioneers and their Descendants*. Berryville, Va.: 1963.

Centennial Year Book: College of Medicine—University of Cincinnati. Cincinnati, 1921.

Chambers, Lenoir. *Stonewall Jackson*. New York: William Morrow & Co., 1959.

Cist, Charles. *Sketches and Statistics of Cincinnati in 1859*. Cincinnati, 1859.

Cresap, Bernarr. *Appomattox Commander; The Story of General E. O. C. Ord*. La Jolla, California: A. S. Barnes and Company, Inc., 1981.

Dammann, Gordon. *Pictorial Encyclopedia of Civil War Medical Instruments and Equipment*. Missoula, Mont.: Pictorial Histories Publishing Company, 1983.

Elliott, Joseph Cantey. *Lieutenant General Richard Heron Anderson: Lee's Noble Soldier*. Dayton, Ohio: Morningside House, Inc., 1985.

Fowler, Silas W. *History of Medicine and Biographical Sketches of the Physicians of Delaware County, Ohio 1804–1910*. Columbus, Ohio: Edward T. Miller Co. for Author, 1910.

Franklin County at the Beginning of the Twentieth Century. Columbus, Ohio: Historical Publishing Company, 1901.

Freeman, Douglas Southall. *Lee's Lieutenants: A Study in Command.* 3 vols. New York: Charles Scribner's Sons, 1946.

Freeman, Douglas Southall. *R. E. Lee: A Biography.* 4 vols. New York: Charles Scribner's Sons, 1935.

Goss, Charles Frederic. *Cincinnati—The Queen City.* 4 vols. Chicago: S. J. Clarke Publishing Company, 1912.

Hassler, Warren W., Jr. *General George B. McClellan: Shield of the Union.* Baton Rouge, La.: Louisiana State University Press, 1957.

History of Delaware County and Ohio. Chicago: O. L. Baskin & Co., 1880.

Johnston, Angus James II. *Virginia Railroads in the Civil War.* Chapel Hill, N.C.: University of North Carolina Press, 1961.

Jones, Virgil Carrington. *Gray Ghosts and Rebel Raiders.* McLean, Va.: EPM Publications, Inc., 1984.

Jones, Virgil Carrington. *Ranger Mosby.* Chapel Hill, N.C.: University of North Carolina Press, 1944.

Juettner, Otto. *Daniel Drake and His Followers: Historical and Biographical Sketches.* Cincinnati: Harvey Publishing Company, 1909.

Lang, Theodore F. *Loyal West Virginia from 1861 to 1865.* Baltimore: Deutsch Publishing Co., 1895.

Lash, Jeffrey N. *Destroyer of the Iron Horse: General Joseph E. Johnston and Confederate Rail Transport, 1861–1865.* Kent, Ohio: Kent State University Press, 1991.

Long, E. B. *The Civil War Day By Day: An Almanac 1861–1865.* Garden City, N.Y.: Doubleday & Company, Inc., 1971.

Mac Master, Richard K. *Augusta County History 1865–1950.* Staunton, Va., 1987.

Morgan, John G. *West Virginia Governors 1863–1980.* Charleston, W. Va.: Charleston Newspapers, 1980.

Morris, George S. & Susan L. Foutz. *Lynchburg in the Civil War.* Lynchburg, Va.: H. E. Howard, Inc., 1984.

Morton, Frederic. *The Story of Winchester in Virginia.* Strasburg, Va.: Shenandoah Publishing House, 1925.

Norris, J. E., ed. *History of the Lower Shenandoah Valley.* Chicago: A. Warner & Co., Publishers, 1890.

O'Connor, Richard. *Sheridan the Inevitable.* Indianapolis: Bobbs-Merrill, 1953.

Peyton, J. Lewis. *History of Augusta County, Virginia.* Bridgewater, Va.: Charles R. Carrier, 1953.

Porter, George H. *Ohio Politics during the Civil War Period.* Repr., New York, 1968.

Powell, Esther Weygandt, comp. *Tombstone Inscriptions and Other Records of Delaware County, Ohio.* Esther Weygandt Powell, 1972.

Quarles, Garland R. *Some Old Homes in Frederick County, Virginia.* Winchester, Va.: Garland Quarles, 1971.

Rawls, Walton, ed. *Great Civil War Heroes and Their Battles*. New York: Abbeville Press, 1985.
Roseboom, Eugene H. *A History of Presidential Elections*. New York: The Macmillan Company, 1957.
Rosenberg, Charles E. *The Trial of the Assassin Guiteau*. Chicago, 1963.
Russell, Charles, ed. *Memoirs of Colonel John S. Mosby*. Bloomington, Ind.: Indiana University Press, 1959.
Scruggs, Philip Lightfoot. *The History of Lynchburg, Virginia 1786–1946*. Lynchburg, Va.: J. P. Bell Co., Inc., n.d.
Shotwell, John B. *A History of the Schools of Cincinnati*. Cincinnati: School Life Co., 1902.
Stackpole, Edward J. *Sheridan in the Shenandoah: Jubal Early's Nemesis*. New York: Bonanza Books, 1961.
Summers, Festus P. *The Baltimore and Ohio in the Civil War*. New York: G. P. Putnam's Sons, 1939.
Waddell, Jos. A. *Annals of Augusta County, Virginia*. Repr.: Harrisonburg, Va.: C. J. Carrier Company, 1979.
Weigley, Russell F. *Quartermaster General of the Union Army: A Biography of M. C. Meigs*. New York: Columbia University Press, 1959.
Wert, Jeffry D. *Mosby's Rangers*. New York: Simon and Schuster, 1990.
Williams, T. Harry. *Lincoln and the Radicals*. New York: Alfred A. Knopf, 1952.
Worthington, Glenn H. *Fighting for Time*. Shippensburg, Pa.: Burd Street Press, 1985.

Articles

Abbot, Maviland Harris, "General John D. Imboden," *West Virginia History* (Jan., 1960), XXI, pp. 88–111.
Bright, Simeon Miller. "The McNeill Rangers: A Study in Confederate Guerilla Warfare," *West Virginia History* (1951), XII, pp. 338–387.
Dooley, Edwin L., Jr. "Lexington in the 1860 Census," *Proceedings of the Rockbridge Historical Society* (Lexington, 1982), IX, pp. 189–196.
Duncan, Richard R. "Maryland's Reaction to Early's Raid in 1864: A Summer of Bitterness," *Maryland Historical Magazine* (Fall, 1969), vol. 64, pp. 248–279.
Eby, Cecil D., Jr. "David Hunter: Villain of the Valley," *Iron Worker* (Spring, 1964), pp. 1–9.
Juettner, Otto. "Rise of Medical Colleges in the Ohio Valley," *Ohio Archaeological and Historical Publications*, vol. 22, pp. 487–489.
Longacre, Edward G. "A Profile of Major General David Hunter," *Civil War Times Illustrated* (Jan., 1978), XVI, pp. 4–9 & 38–43.
Schenck, Robert C. "Major-General David Hunter," *Magazine of American History* (New York, 1887), XVII, pp. 138–152.

Tucker, David A., Jr. "Some Early Landmarks in the Medical History of Cincinnati," *The Ohio State Medical Journal*, vol. 18 (Jan, 1942), pp. 55–58.

Wert, Jeffry. "The Woodstock Races," *Civil War Times Illustrated*, XIX (May, 1980), pp. 8–12.

White, Robert. "West Virginia," in *Confederate Military History* (Repr., The Blue and Grey Press), VII, pp. 1–138.

Index

133

Leesburg, Va., 49, 50
Letcher, Governor John, 36, 52, 112n. 70, 119n. 22
Lexington, Va., 2, 9, 35, 37, 52, 104n. 20, 112n. 70, 114nn. 77, 79
Libby Prison, 14, 95
Liberty, Va., 9
Lincoln, Abraham, 14, 95, 100n. 1, 105n. 23, 107n. 42, 109n. 59, 110n. 59, 119nn. 14, 21, 120n. 23, 125n. 10
Lincoln, Lieutenant Colonel William S., 32, 109n. 58, 110n. 60, 112n. 70, 114n. 77
Livermore, Thomas L., 123n. 53
Lomax, Major General Lunsford, 122n. 48, 124n. 66
London, England, x, 101nn. 5, 6
Longstreet, Lieutenant General James, 28, 58, 109n. 52, 120n. 26
Lookout Mountain, Battle of, 4
Louisa Court House, Va., 44, 116n. 1
Loudon County, Va., 122n. 50
Lynch, Charles H., 114n. 77
Lynchburg, Va., 2, 5, 8, 9, 35-37, 40, 44, 52, 57, 75, 97, 104nn. 20, 21, 111n. 61, 112n. 70, 114nn. 79, 80, 115nn. 80, 81, 83, 116n. 85

M

McCausland, Brigadier General John, 85, 112n. 71, 115n. 81, 119n. 22, 120n. 22
McClellan, Major General George B. 2, 62-63, 106n. 36, 121n. 33
McDowell, Brigadier General Irwing, 1
McIntosch, Brigadier General John Baillie, 121n. 42
McLean, Wilmer, 99
McMaster, Charles, 122n. 51
McNeill, Captain John, 108n. 48
Manassas, First Battle of, 108n. 51, 109n. 59, 113n. 74
Manassas, Second Battle of, 2
Manassas Gap Railroad, 122n. 47
Manassas Junction, 70
Marion County, W.Va., 102n. 6
Marky, Harry, 56
Marshall County, W.Va., 102n. 6
Martinsburg, W.Va., 5, 20-23, 26-28, 31-32, 35, 45-49, 51, 54-55, 70-72, 74, 83, 85, 103n. 2, 106nn. 37, 41, 42, 107n. 42, 108n. 45, 110n. 59, 118n. 7

Maryland, 1, 2, 9, 42, 45-46, 48, 104n. 22, 105n. 26, 107n. 43, 117n. 3, 118n. 7, 119n. 18
Maryland Heights, 54-57, 118n. 7
Mason, 40
Massanutten Gap, 6, 83, 103n. 2
Massanutten Mountain, 120n. 27
Maxwell, Daniel, 14
Meade, Major General George, 5, 8
Meaney, Peter J., 119n. 15
Means, Lieutenant Thomas H., 13, 105n. 27
Medical College of Ohio, viii, 101n. 5, 102n. 5
Medical Department of University of Cincinnati, 102n. 5
Meigs, Lieutenant John R., 68, 111n. 65, 122nn. 45, 50
Mercer, Ella, 12
Merritt, Wesley, 83, 122n. 50, 124n. 66
Mexican War, 109n. 59
Mexico, ix, 95
Miami Medical College, 102n. 5
Middle Department, 114n. 74
Middle Military Division, 77, 83, 120n. 24
Middlebourne, W.Va., 100n. 1
Middletown, Va., 74, 119n. 16, 124n. 66
Miles, Lynes, 19
Milroy, Major General Robert, 2, 26, 105n. 31
Mississippi Valley Medical Association, x
Mississippi River, vii
Missouri, Mo., 105n. 23, 110n. 59
Monocacy, Battle of, 117n. 3
Monocacy Junction, 105n. 26, 117n. 3, 120n. 23
Monocacy River, 45, 117n. 3
Moor, Colonel Augustus, 6, 7, 103n. 10
Moore Frederick Gambrill, 106n. 39
Moore, Gibbons, 106n. 39
Moore, Jane Boswell, 21, 27, 106n. 39
Moorefield, W.Va., 105n. 24, 124n. 62
Morgan, General Daniel, 88
Morrison, Frances Henderson, 113n. 72
Mosby, Colonel John Singleton, 78, 122nn. 50, 51, 123n. 57
Mount Crawford, Va., 8, 104n. 18, 122n. 43
Mount Jackson, Va., 6, 8, 28-29, 31-32, 86, 111n. 61, 122n. 47
Mulligan, Colonel James A., 46, 54, 188n. 7

N

Nashville, Battle of, 124n. 68
Nashville, Tenn., 124n. 63
Natural Bridge, 47
Neil, Alexander, vii-x, 93-96, 101n. 5, 102nn. 12, 14, 107n. 42, 124n. 3
Neil, Charles Wesley, viii, 101nn. 2, 3
Neil, Dessie, 102n. 12
Neil, Gamma, 102n. 12
Neil, Goldie, 102n. 12
Neil, James, 63-64, 76, 78, 82, 101n. 3
Neil, John, 12-13, 18, 51, 58, 60, 69, 85, 101n. 3, 105n. 29
Neil, Sattie, 13, 51, 85
Neil, William, 41, 56, 62, 64-65, 90-91
New Castle, Pa., 88, 90
New Creek, W.Va., 10, 85, 108n. 48, 124n. 62
New Market, Battle of, ix, 1, 28, 32, 35, 56, 108n. 50, 109n. 57, 110n. 59
New Market, Va., 6-8, 28, 77, 86, 89, 124n. 66
New River bridge, 5, 112n. 69, 113n. 73
Newtown (Stephen City), Va., 58, 70, 72, 74-80, 83, 120n. 25
New York, N.Y., 104n. 23
Nineteenth Army Corps, 50-51, 56-57, 59, 66-67, 72, 87, 90
Ninety-First Ohio Infantry, 52
North Anna, Battle of, 111n. 62
North Mountain, 79, 121n. 41
North River, 4, 8, 111n. 65, 112nn. 70, 71
Northcott, Robert S., 14, 105n. 30
Northern Neck of Virginia, 124n. 65

O

Odbert, Charles H., 12
Ohio, ix-x, 10, 47, 91
Ohio River, 100n. 1
Ohio Wesleyan University, viii, 101n. 3
One Hundred and Sixteenth Ohio Infantry, 110n. 60
One Hundred and Twenty-Third Ohio Infantry, 32
Opequon Creek, 63-65, 67, 76, 121nn. 34, 37
Orange and Alexandria Railroad, 4, 44, 115n. 80
Ord, Major General Edward O. C., 17, 93, 98, 106n. 35

P

Page (Luray) Valley, 6, 124n. 66
Parkersburg, W.Va., 40, 46-47, 52, 100n. 1, 118n. 13
Parkersburg, W. Va., *Gazette*, 118n. 13
Patterson, William, 114n. 77
Pea Ridge, Battle of, 105n. 23
Peaks of Otter, 8-9, 47
Pennsylvania, vii, 1-2, 45, 56, 107n. 43, 119n. 18
Petersburg, Va., 46, 91, 93-94, 97-98, 104n. 21, 115n. 80
Petersburg, W.Va., 10, 105n. 24
Philadelphia, Pa., 75
Philippi, Battle of, 104n. 22, 106n. 36
Philippi House, 16
"Philippi Races," 106n. 34
Philippi, W.Va., 16-20
Piedmont, Battle of, 34-35, 42, 68, 111n. 64
Piedmont, Va., 8, 85, 108n. 48, 124n. 62
Piedmont, W.Va., 27
Pierpont, Governor Francis, 95, 125n. 9
Pierpont, Francis H., Jr., 13, 105n. 27
Pierpont, Major Francis Perry, 124n. 3
Pigott, Lieutenant Elam F., 12, 105n. 25
Pleasant Valley, Md., 56, 58, 64
Point of Rocks, Md., 49
Port Republic, Va., 34, 68
"Porte Crayon," 105n. 23
Potomac River, 2, 42, 45, 55, 59, 60, 65, 75, 115n. 81, 119nn. 16, 18, 120n. 28
Potomac River, North Branch, 46
Potomac River, South Branch, 105n. 24
Powell, William H., 124n. 66
Pritchard, Captain Amos H., 15

R

Randolph County, W.Va., 17
Rappahannock-Rapidan Line, vii, 1-2
Ramseur, Major General Stephen D., 44
Reams' Station, 121n. 31
Red River, 110n. 59
Reid, James H., 51
Republican Party, 101n. 1
Rhodes, D. W., vii
Rich Mountain, 17, 106n. 36
Richards, Minnie, 19, 69, 88, 90
Richmond, Va., ix, 2, 4-5, 15, 27, 34-35, 44, 46, 62, 67, 81, 83, 85, 89, 93-96, 100n. 1, 105nn. 24, 28, 106n. 31, 108n. 47, 111n. 63, 115nn. 80, 81, 125n. 9